GREETINGS
TO OUR FRIENDS
IN BRAZIL

PAUL DURCAN's first book of poems, *Endsville* (with Brian Lynch) was published in 1967 and has been followed by fifteen others, including *Daddy, Daddy* (Winner of the Whitbread Award for Poetry, 1990) and *A Snail in My Prime: New and Selected Poems* (1993). His most recent book is the long poem, *Christmas Day* (1996). He is a member of Aosdána and lives in Dublin.

Paul Durcan

GREETINGS TO OUR FRIENDS IN BRAZIL

One Hundred Poems

THE HARVILL PRESS

LONDON

First published in Great Britain in 1999 by
The Harvill Press
2 Aztec Row, Berners Road
London N1 0PW

www.harvill-press.com

1 3 5 7 9 8 6 4 2

A CIP catalogue record for this title
is available from the British Library

ISBN 1 86046 607 9 (hbk)
ISBN 1 86046 638 9 (pbk)

Designed and typeset in Bembo at
Libanus Press, Marlborough, Wiltshire

Printed and bound in Great Britain by Butler & Tanner Ltd
at Selwood Printing, Burgess Hill

TO ANTHONY CRONIN
POET
CRITIC, ESSAYIST, NOVELIST, HISTORIAN
WHO WHILE MANY OF US CHATTERED
GOT THINGS DONE THAT MATTERED
FRIEND, COMRADE, COMPANION
WITH ABIDING AFFECTION

ACKNOWLEDGEMENTS

To Aosdána and the Arts Council of the Republic of Ireland
without whose support this book could not have been written,
my deepest thanks.
I should also like to thank the British Council
and the Arts Council of England.

Versions of eight of these poems were published in the news pages
of the *Sunday Independent*. Versions of seven other poems appeared
in *Céide*, *Force 10*, the *London Review of Books*, the *Irish Times*.
"Self-Portrait as an Irish Jew" appeared in *At the Edge of the
Edge of Mark Joyce* (Green on Red Gallery, 1998).

I wish to record my gratitude to the family of the late Heinrich Böll,
the Achill Heinrich Böll Committee, Mayo County Council,
and Mr Michael Carr.

To Bernard and Mary Loughlin at the Tyrone Guthrie Centre,
again and again, thank you for close on twenty years a-welcoming.

For advice and support of divers kinds I wish to thank Donal McCann,
Kathleen McCracken, Patrick Nugent, Gerald Owens,
Síabhra Durcan and Sarah Durcan.

Any author who has the good fortune to have had Bill Swainson
as an editor will know the debt I owe him. In the case of this book,
however, he has invested time and effort beyond the call of duty.

I wish also to salute Alice Maher whose drawing
Coma Berenices (The Love-Knot), which appears on the cover and
on each of the part-title pages, has been for me the single most
satisfying event in the composition of this book.

First and last, my gratitude to Kate Sweetman.

CONTENTS

What one seems to want in art, in experiencing it, is the same thing that is necessary for its creation, a self-forgetful, perfectly useless concentration.

ELIZABETH BISHOP

Greetings to Our Friends in Brazil

I

On the Friday night before the last Sunday in September
I got a phone call from Father Patrick O'Brien, CC, in
    Kilmeena, Co Mayo
Inviting me to drive over to his house on Sunday afternoon
And watch the All Ireland Football Final on television,
Mayo against Kerry.
He told me that he had to say the eleven o'clock Mass in
    Kilmeena
But that after Mass he would be free for the day:
We could drive into Westport, have lunch at the Asgard on
    the Quay,
Drive back to his house in time to watch the match.

His invitation solved the problem of the weekend.
I was staying thirty miles away in Dugort on Achill Island
In a cottage with no television – an ex-soldier's outpost
On the side of a mountain – a German soldier
Who had fought on both fronts.
Like everyone else in Mayo and Kerry
I was keen to see the match. On the Saturday night
After answering a pile of letters –
After slicing the top off the pile –
I went to my bed an expectant, contented man –
Army surplus bed, cast-iron frame, wire springs.
Tomorrow would be a day of affection as well as of rest:
An authentic Sabbath;
No politics;
No jealousy or rivalry;
Lunch and conversation with a compatible man;

And in the Asgard on Westport Quay!
I'd never been in the Asgard before!
And then the centrepiece of the day, the highlight of the year,
    the big match.
Watching it in the comfort of the fireside of Father O'Brien's
    study.
Coasting sleepwards I got to thinking –
If I manage to get up at any kind of reasonably early hour
    tomorrow
I might also catch beforehand the eleven o'clock Mass.

II

As I drove up the hill to Kilmeena parish church – the holy
    mountain
Of Croagh Patrick asleep on its back on the skyline in blue
    pencil outline –
God on his back asleep under a haycock –
Early-morning elders out on the golf links at Carraholly –
Their seminaked wives in sunglasses in patio chairs –
All the Susannahs of Fahy –
The bell was tolling three minutes to eleven.
I jumped out of the car, not even bothering to lock it.
Not even bothering to roll up the driver's window.
I felt like a man without a care in the world.

I was surprised by the atmosphere in the chapel:
Devout but without
The normal social hypocrisies of Sunday church attendance.
Country people engrossed in the present tense:
Stallion with mare; mare with foal;
Cocks on the verges of fantasies;
All the hens in their pews cackling "Shhsh-shhsh";
Ultra-orthodox guinea hens negatively not shrieking;
Geese in their grey greatness;

4

The future not a chimera but a possibility;
The past not a millstone but a life raft.
All of us being toasted by electric fires high up on the walls:
All of us gazing altarwards at the stained glass window of
    Mother and Child –
The Gold Madonna of Mayo.

The bell tolls again, the congregation stands up,
Enter the tiny procession
Of three altar boys in white surplices
Being shepherded by the celebrant in green-and-red chasuble.
The stocky quiet man I had known for twenty years
In that instant became a prophet of the Lord.
He shed his years and spoke in a strong voice –
A young, lifeboat coxswain's voice
Reeking of daring;
Every inflection, every gesture
Effected a rescue of innocence:
Not so much as an iota of unctuousness
Or melodrama or power-tripping or patronage
Or Uncle Tomming or craw-thumping or Musha, God Help Us.

III

It was the Twenty-Sixth Sunday in Ordinary Time.
A small boy read from The Book of Numbers:
How the spirit came down on two men who missed Mass –
Eldad and Medad. "Me Dad" the little boy pronounced it.
"If only the whole people of the Lord were prophets,
And the Lord gave his Spirit to them all."
A small girl read from the letter of St James:
A message for the well-off;
"On earth you have had a life of comfort and luxury;
In the time of slaughter you went on eating to your heart's
    content.

5

It was you who condemned the innocent and killed them:
They offered you no resistance."

Father O'Brien climbed up into the pulpit.
In the cadences of the shoulders
Of the dead fishermen of the islands of Mayo –
The drowned kings of the roads of Clew Bay –
He read out his sermon:
The sheepdogs of his words pricking their ears
To the pitch of his soul's whistling;
Slow, easy-going, rope-narrow cadences
Humping on their broad, gleaming shoulders
Hundreds of little children with big, wide eyes;
The sprightly and the retarded;
Every time I looked up at Father O'Brien
He seemed to be getting younger by the paragraph.
He looked like a drowning man who had no fear of drowning;
His enthusiasm tipping its red forelock to nobody;
The cliff-high, forest-roaring, tiger-snarling sea
Of rip currents cowered under his words.

He spoke of his friend who had died in a plane crash, John
     Feeney:
Of how when John Feeney had been editor of *The Irish Catholic*
His editorials had so displeased the Archbishop of Dublin –
His Grace John Charles McQuaid –
Feeney plagiarized the letter of St James for his next editorial;
St James would be an imprimatur
That would not only suffice but impress;
Copied it verbatim but without quotation marks.
The Archbishop of Dublin slashed a red marker pen through
     the entire editorial.
James – Father O'Brien told us – is the leading editorial of
     Christianity.

IV

We had a good, honest lunch in the Asgard sitting up at the bar:
Chowder, plaice, chips, whiskey, ginger ale, coffee.
Invoking old friends; Tony O'Malley, Brendan Kennelly,
    John Moriarty.
We got back to his house in good time for the preliminaries:
The teams one by one tumbling out onto the park –
Young bulls in their groiny primes
Charging out the tunnel into the arena of their fate.
Bouncing up and down in the silky greensward.
Trying out their tails; bucking their butts.
Draining their nostrils; tossing their horns.
Spitting. Sniffing. Swearing.
Revving. Jiving. Cartwheeling.
The teams getting their photographs taken;
The parade, the mime-singing of the national anthem.
Father O'Brien lit a turf fire and brought in a tray of coffee;
The four walls of his study decorated
With photographs and postcards and prints
And paintings with antiquely wrought cobwebs on their frames,
And the blinds drawn, and the television working.

Getting good television pictures, we turned down the volume –
The diligent Ger Canning churning out clichés –
And, marrying radio sound to television picture,
We tuned in to the radio commentary
By the cordial Kerry maestro Mícheál Ó Muircheartaig.
"We send greetings to you all from Djakarta down to Crossmolina
And the ball goes to Kenneth Mortimer having a great game
    for Mayo
He has a brother doing research work on the Porcupine Bank
But now it goes to Killian Burns of Kerry
The best accordion-playing cornerback in football today.
We hope you're on the astra if you're in outer space.

On my watch it says two minutes and fifty- three seconds left but
We haven't had time to send greetings to our friends in Brazil
Proinnsias O Murchu and Rugierio da Costa e Silva."

We watched our native Mayo get defeated yet again,
Commiserated with each other.
A few last parting words about Steiner's *Errata*,
George Steiner's autobiography
Which Father O'Brien had read on the Westport train on
    Wednesday.
Father O'Brien whispered: "He's very good on Israel."
I blurted: "Can you recommend a commentary on the Bible?"
Father O'Brien put his finger to his lips and ran upstairs
And came running back downstairs with a disintegrating tome:
"If it is any use to you, you can borrow my Jerome."
He walked me to my car in the grave-digging rain,
Clouds with broad black brushes
Smearing the white vellum of the sky,
Gales brewing their hysterias.
Wishing each other well for the winter months ahead.
Counselling one another with tears and smiles.
Encouraging one another.
See you again next summer.
We embraced goodbye.

v

On the Siberian, Saharan, Gobi drive back to Achill Island
I stopped at Burrishoole to give a lift
To a small, middle-aged woman standing alone
On the edge of the road in the grieving storm.
She looked like a bat at nightfall in a doorway
Under the lintel hovering
"In darkness and secrecy and loneliness".

Her arranged lift had fallen through.
She said: Do you mind if I smoke?
I said: I don't mind at all.
Actually, I minded fearfully:
Cigarette smoke nauseates me in the gut.
She was smoking Sweet Afton
The name of which I have to admit I do savour.
She also had been watching the match but to my consternation
Far from being dejected she was cheerful –
Cheerful for having watched it. We discussed players.
She furling and unfurling her green-and-red scarf;
Fondling her green-and-red flag in her lap.
We agreed Kenneth Mortimer had a powerful game.
The sensitive subject of Liam MacHale had barely been broached
Before the rain teemed so hard I could not see out the
    windscreen –
My wipers flailing in ecstatic futility –
And I had to stop the car in the middle of a red bog that looked
As if it were turning white in the storm.
She put a hand on my shoulder and a little finger on my cheek.
She smiled: I hope you don't mind me saying so
But you have got a bushy left eyebrow and there seems
To be a baby spider caught up in the fibres.

I said: Thank you.
She said: I hope you don't mind me saying so but you look
    quite depressed.
I said: I take Seroxat.
She said: Never mind the Seroxat.
I said: Do I look that bad?
She said: Look at me!
I said: I'm looking at you.
She announced: I'm destitute!
She smiled the wry grimace of an angel in Los Angeles

Who's been around in the western world for a long time:
A smile as accustomed to a fireside chair
As to a hard wooden bench against the wall;
A smile only the tippy-toes of whose feet
Are apparent at the end of the couch;
A smile with which you cannot tell
Whether the smiler is laughing or crying;
A smile bent double in January woods
In long, blue, denim skirt,
White blouse, black stockings,
Black patent leather shoes,
Long, black overcoat,
Picking posies of snowdrops
For brave, nameless women in mortal combat with cancer;
For brave, nameless men in mortal combat with cancer.

I drove on and she didn't speak again for the rest of the journey.
At the bend in the road outside Achill Sound she asked to get out.
Glancing up at the sky, she remarked: Himself is at home –
I have a whole family to feed and to clothe.
I said: Boys or girls? She said: Seven girls and two boys.
I dug thumb and forefinger into my breast pocket
And fished out a note.
Hovering in the shelter of a small oak with rhododendrons
     she said:
Goodbye. God bless – I said. God bless you – she said.
For the remaining nine miles I held on to the driving wheel
As if it were the microphone on the bridge of a ship
     going down;
Going over the tops of the crests of the blanket bogs;
Navigating Bunnacurry, Gowlawaum, Bogach Bawn;
Muttering as if my life depended on it:
Greetings to our friends in Brazil.

Landed in the German soldier's cottage
On the side of the big mountain
Between the mountain stream and the roadside fuchsia
I light a turf fire and sit on the sofa
With my hands joined across my stomach.
On the last Sunday in September
For the first time in years
I feel no craving:
Not for food not for drink not for anything.
Not for grapes.
Not for newspaper not for book.
Not for radio not for television not for telephone.
I hear the tempest o'er the mountains and the seas.
I hear the silence of the spheres.
I see two hundred million pairs of shut eyes
Of two hundred million sleeping faces
Behind two hundred million windows in the warring night.
Only the dead are not homeless.
Each to their layers of skins.
Each to caravans on hard edges.
Each to their pigeonhole in the dovecote.
Each to their breeze-block in the estate.
Each to their liftshaft in the tower block.
Each to their cardboard in the doorway.
Each to their roost in the ashram.
Each to their cabin on the mountain.
I hear sheep baa-baaing to sheep on the mountainside:
Genocide, genocide.
I hear ravens diving the peaks:
Ethnic cleansing, ethnic cleansing.
I hear tied-up terriers barking:
Thoughtlessness, thoughtlessness.

I hear Father O'Brien at my side at my
ear:
His exegesis of the word "mercy" –
Its Aramaic etymology;
"Mercy is by definition exclusively divine.
Mercy is a divine, not a human term."
I feel ready to go to bed.
Let me pray:
Greetings to our friends in Brazil.

25 OCTOBER 1997

Recife Children's Project, 10 June 1995

Crèche Nossa Senhora Dos Remedios
Inaugurada Com Missa Solene Por
Dom Helder Camara
No Dia 22 De Outubro De 1978

On a Saturday afternoon in Recife, humid, grey,
An aimiable Englishman, Eddie Edmundson,
A linguist whose father was a clogger in Clitheroe –
"An eddy of semantic scruples" he was later to say –
Drove me out into the suburbs and shantytowns
To visit Father Frank Murphy, Holy Ghost missionary,
Founder of the Recife Children's Project:
A seventy-year-old County Wexford priest
Who has organized a school for the children of mothers
Who have no choice but to work on the streets
Selling their bodies for shelter and food.
Father Murphy was proud of his *crèche* –
That's what he calls it, his *crèche* –
But mostly what he wanted to talk about was poetry.

In the dying day darkening by the edges
Of a concrete pond of black, red-headed swans
In virgin jungle in northwest Recife
That aged, placid Wexfordman lifted his sore head
Skywards past coconut trees, quoting
In all its meticulous intricacy,
"Rage for Order" by Derek Mahon.
When he had done, giving the thumbs-up sign,
He put his hand on my shoulder:
"This is what we do in Brazil."

Driving back into the *centro* of Recife
Past "scorched gable ends and burnt-out buses"
We drove in silence until I declared
"We have spent this afternoon with Che Guevara."
Eddie the Englishman said: "Yes . . .
Yes, I know exactly what you mean, you are right."
Father Frank Murphy, Founder of the Recife Children's
    Project,
Thirty years working in the streets of Recife,
For whom poetry is reality, reality poetry,
Who does not carry a gun,
Who does not prattle about politics or religion,
Whose sign is the thumbs-up sign of Brazil,
Who puts his hand on your shoulder saying
"This is what we do in Brazil."
Che? Frank!
No icon he —
Revolutionary hero of the twentieth century.

The Last Shuttle to Rio

to Patrick Early

It's been a bad day in São Paulo.

Paulistas have a saying –
"Life is a game of the hips"
But today my hips have had a bad game.
My knees have been up to the mark
But my hips have been pathetic.

Standing up at the counter of the café
In the airport at Congonhas,
Stirring my coffee with my right hand,
Holding my mobile phone in my left hand,
I am whispering to my publisher;
Whispering in low, steadfast, tightlipped whines
"Why were my books not there?"
"Where were my books?"
"Why was Ivan Kerr in Belo Horizonte
When he was supposed to be in São Paulo?"

Through the condensed perspiration of my hysterical whispers
I discern a small, lean, nine-year-old black boy
With a shoebox on his shoulder pointing down at my shoes.
Yet another intrusion in a day of multiple intrusions.
I bounce my skull angrily: *Sim, sim, sim.*
Hopping the ball of my skull off the tiled floor of my anger.

I resume berating my publisher
Immediately erasing from my mind

The shoeshine boy kneeling at my feet
Until I feel a tapping at my knee.
What do you want now?
He wants my left foot.
He's done with my right.

I glimpse the frills of his jet black hair.
They are perfect frills –
Perfectly formed pasta frills.
What a shine he is giving me!
For the first time today
I feel a pang of wellbeing.

All the while he is polishing me
He is watching me
With hot, scooped eyes staring up
Out of his yellow T-shirt
Inscribed PACIFIC WAVES.
I am no longer abusing
My hurting publisher.
The shoeshine boy is sprinting.
He is putting his right arm into it.
Putting everything into his right arm.
Putting everything into his rag.

He leaps to his feet.
He has finished. He squashes
A coke tin in his small fist.
I beg my publisher's forgiveness.
I hang up,
Clipping my mobile
Back on to my hip.
I thank him for giving me
Such a brilliant shine.

I say: "Obrigado."
He replies with a shy shrug:
"De nada."

My God, you have made
My day in São Paulo
And you have the audacity
To reply "De nada".

With your shoebox on your shoulder
You repeat with unconditional candour
"De nada"
Gazing up unblinking into my eyes.

I stutter: "What is your name?"
Out of your mouth-womb
Leaps your divine name:
"Einstein! Einstein João Luis Soares!"

Fernando's Wheelbarrows, Copacabana

FERNANDO'S WHEELBARROWS, COPACABANA
are at Rua Vinicius de Moraes 208
at the Ipanema end of Copacabana

Akimbo in a wheelbarrow in Copacabana
I am a gringo sober as a judge –
Grey-souled as my father who was a judge.
I am waiting for Fernando
To wheel me up and down the beach.
Fernando does not speak a word of English
Nor I of Portuguese.
Fernando's forebears were slaves from Senegal.
Fernando is a free man, proudest of the proud.

Because Fernando believes that good manners
Are the highest grade of ethical behaviour –
That is an article of faith with Fernando –
I have requested that Fernando
Be my guide in Copacabana:
My guide, my governor, my master.

Every evening at seven o'clock after Mass
Fernando wheels me up and down the beach
At Copacabana in the silence of the dead;
Fernando is the silentest man in Copacabana
Just as I am the silentest man in Dublin.
Our climaxes are meeting and parting.
I rejoice in the remote way Fernando shakes my
    hand.
I rejoice in the comotose stars of Fernando's eyes.
I rejoice in the reticence of Fernando's laughter.

The only time Fernando breaks his silence
Is at the midpoint of our giro;
Fernando reveals to me his dream
Of emigrating to Phoenix, Arizona.
Fernando has a young wife and children.
He explains by means of his hands
And by two words – Phoenix, Arizona.
His hands with rhetorical ebullience exhort:
Phoenix, Arizona is the good life!

Samambaia

Living in the clouds in Brazil
Or living in the clouds in Ireland
Is vast of a vastness –

Fern
Behind whose face paint
My Indian eyes blink.

Night is day:
Nothing stays the same.
Everything changes.

Sunlight is rain:
Nothing should stay the same.
Everything should change.

If you love her
You will never
Take her for granted

Nor will you think twice
If the choice
Is between love and fame.

I, Elizabeth,
Do take you, Lota,
For my lawful, wedded cloud.

The Geography of Elizabeth Bishop

There is a life before birth
On earth – oh yes, on earth –
And it is called Brazil.
Call it paradise, if you will.

Reared in New England, Nova Scotia,
I was orphaned in childhood.
Despite the fastidiousness of aunts
I could know myself only as an alien –
An authority of courtesy –
Until aged forty on a voyage round Cape Horn
I stepped off in Rio, stayed, discovered
My mind in Brazil. Became again an *infanta*!
A thinking monkey's *companero*!
Fed, cuddled, above all needed.
In the treetops of Samambaia
I made a treehouse;
In Ouro Prêto I made a nest
In a niche in a cliff in a valley
Of nineteen golden churches.

At forty I discovered that my voice –
That cuckoo hymen of mine, mine, mine –
Was a Darwinian tissue:
That in God's *cinéma vérité*
I was an authentic *bocadinho*.

Back in Boston, a late-middle-aged lady,
I became again an orphan,
Put on orphan uniform,

Endured the timetable of the orphanage –
All these invigilators sliding
In and out their Venetian blinds
With not a baby elephant in sight
Nor chimp nor toucan nor parakeet.
I stilled the pain with alcohol
And with self-pity – in spite
Of which, death waxed merciful.

> *There is a life before birth*
> *On earth – oh yes, on earth –*
> *And it is called Brazil.*
> *Call it paradise, if you will.*

Casa Mariana Trauma

Under her window in Ouro Prêto
She is wringing locutions, wringing shrunken,
Faded, threadbare words
To squeeze oil paint out of tubes of language:
The trauma of the painter as the poet.

The Who's Who of American Poetry

Who *is* Elizabeth Bishop?
She is the Patrick Kavanagh of Rio de Janeiro.
A ring-a-rosied mudlark under the flyover;
A missing vagrant in the homeless halo.

Televised Poetry Encounter, Casa Fernando Pessoa, Lisboa

to Manuela Judice and Casimiro de Brito

I

"We have these weeks in Lisboa
At the Casa Fernando Pessoa
The Irish poet Mr Paul Durcan.
Senhor, what means it to be
The Irish poet of the twentieth century?"

"The puzzle is to be in Lisboa
At the Casa Fernando Pessoa.
To be the Irish poet of the twentieth century
Is to be – how can I find the words? –
Is to be an Irishman playing for England in Brazil!"

II

"Born Paul Durcan
In '44
I began,
When I was eleven
In '56
And unearthing
The goldmine of my body,
To undergo
A change
Of name.

At eleven
I was in heaven

With passion
For romance
And sport,
Theatre and blue jeans,
Religion and film,
Les Enfants du Paradis,
Black Orpheus,
Climbing mountains
In search
Of beautiful women,
Being a wild
Colonial Balthus.
Anything not to be
A tame Brian Ryan.

Oh in time
Of Coca-Cola
And Pelé,
Michael MacLiammóir
And Jayne Mansfield,
I became –
Tinkerly Luxemburgo.

I write
Under the pen name
Paul Durcan
But my real name –
Like Balthus
Or William Trevor –
Is Tinkerly Luxemburgo."

Tinkerly Luxemburgo
1944–1999
I will lift up mine eyes unto the hills:
from whence cometh my help.

Elvira Tulip, Annaghmakerrig

Elvira Tulip is loitering on a grass bank above me
In a blue swimsuit, explaining to me what it means
To be experimental – Virginia Woolf, Samuel Beckett –

While behind her strides
The Steward of Annaghmakerrig humming in Catalan:
Where would I be without my wheelbarrow?

I am standing under her down in the gravel
Clad from head to foot – jeans, T-shirt,
Jumper, trainers – blinking up at her,

My young teacher, my young virtuoso,
My idea, my reality, my dance, my fix
On the cosmos as it is late in the afternoon.

Where would I be without my wheelbarrow?
My wheelbarrow that's got two handles and one very small
  rubber wheel.
Is there not one woman in the world who would marry me
  for my wheelbarrow?

The Daring Middle-Aged Man
on the Flying Trapeze

to Munira Mutran

The sort of travel I'm into nowadays in São Paulo
Is going to bed early with my wife,
Staying in bed late in the mornings with my wife.
However, when I heard that on June 16
In Finnegans Pub in São Paulo
A Japanese actor would be declaiming in Portuguese
Extracts from *Ulysses*
My wife persuaded me to fly with her to Dublin.
I remonstrated with her: "Fly?"
She insisted: "Dublin is a gas,
Dirty, ordinary, transcendental city – just like São Paulo!"

We stayed in the YWCA in Sandymount –
Radcliffe Hall in St John's Road:
£13 per person sharing for a chalet
In the rose garden behind the Hall.
I liked the Hall because it was beside
Not only the Martello Tower on Sandymount Strand
But the Church of Ireland in St John's Road
Which is so C of E
It makes the Roman Catholic Church
On the far side of Sandymount Village –
The Star of the Sea –
Appear Low – so very Low!
Myself, I am Brazilian Armenian Orthodox.
(Last year I had some of my ashes buried in Armenia
After my left leg was amputated below the knee

Following an accident during Carnaval –
A loose nut on my trapeze.)

I liked Radcliffe Hall most of all for the rose garden:
Kingsize, queensize double beds of roses;
Red roses, white roses, yellow roses.
At midnight – 9 p.m. São Paulo time –
We sat out in the rose garden under a Howth moon
Listening to motor traffic – the Japanese actor
Declaiming *Ulysses* in Portuguese
In Finnegans Pub in São Paulo –
The rose petals staggering off their stems.

I sat with my hands on my knees
(I have still got my *two* knees)
Thinking how simple a thing peace is
In spite of man's addiction to war.
Although I am a middle-aged man on one leg,
When my wife asked –
Will you walk me along Sandymount Strand –
Actually, what she said was
"Let's check out the modality of the visible" –
I said "Yes" and I saw her –
I saw her quite simply, clearly, wholly –
Skip down the strand ahead of me,
Her meagre, white blouse billowing,
Her brown shoulders gleaming.
I thought:
James Joyce is the only man in the world who comprehends
    women;
Who comprehends that a woman can never be adumbrated,
Properly praised
Except by a Japanese actor
In Finnegans Pub in São Paulo
Declaiming extracts from *Ulysses.*

Brazilian Presbyterian

Ten days ago in Fortaleza,
Evandro – a young
Brazilian Presbyterian –
Drove me to the sea.
In a country with a population
Of two hundred million
There was no one
To be seen at the sea.

I sat on the dune
Under a coconut tree;
Diving in and out
Of the South Atlantic;
At fifty years of age
A nipper in excelsis.

Driving back into Fortaleza
I put the question to Evandro:
How would you – a young
Brazilian Presbyterian –
Imagine heaven?

Driving on in silence,
Caressing the steering wheel
Of his Space Wagon,
The Brazilian Presbyterian
Began to think aloud:
"Heaven . . . is a place . . .
That . . . would *surprise* you."

Jack Lynch

to Mike Murphy

Jack Lynch is an accountant in Rio.
Born in São Paulo in 1939
Of a first generation Brazilian, middle-class father from
    Ballinasloe
Who was devoured by a mulatto working-class goddess.
His father had him christened Jack because he liked the black
    look of him.
If he hadn't liked the black look of him he'd have called him
    Claude.
(His father divided up the human race into Jacks and Claudes.)
Jack made his home in Rio thirty-odd years ago.

Nothing happens in Rio that Jack Lynch doesn't know about.
Yesterday I sat with him in a cardboard shack
In a shantytown in Rio and listened to him
Tell the wide-eyed chisellers about his own daughter
Jumping off the top of Corcovado.
(His daughter is a champion hang-glider.)
He shakes his head, holding back the tears:
"I can't say I'm not proud of her."
The slum kids offer him handfuls of grime
Crying out to him – tell us it again.

Today it's the same story.
Only this time we're on the patio
Of the private members' bar
At the Golf Clube 10 kilometres west of Rio
Gazing up at yet another Sugar Loaf mountain
With yet another shantytown adhering to its precipices
And from whose peak his daughter

Has jumped off in her hang-glider.
Back in Rio at twilight walking the Red Beach
Under the Sugar Loaf mountain at Urca
Just when I think there's nothing more
He can tell me about his hang-gliding daughter
He points a finger up at a cliff-rim –
His daughter has been known to ride a motorbike
Along the edge of the cliff.

Jack, what do you mean –
"Along the edge of the cliff"?
He explains about a two-foot wide rim.
Anyway . . . that's another thing his daughter does:
She rides motorbikes along narrow spaces
On the tops of things – cliffs, roofs, parapets.
It's not just that Jack Lynch lives on another planet:
It's that Jack Lynch is himself another planet.
Jack Lynch is a Brazilian who lives in Brazil.
The slum kids offer him handfuls of grime
Crying out to him – tell us it again.

A Visitor from Rio de Janeiro

Maria Teresa has nipped over from Rio de Janeiro to visit me.
I say "nipped over":
Yesterday she drove to school in the University of Rio de Janeiro.
Today she is striding out with me along Sandymount Strand.

A man – a sea-faring man –
In an off-white mac
Sauntering past us
Sings out my name.
Twice he sings out my name.
"Durcaninho! Durcaninho!"

It is the poet Mahon.
Captain of my nation
Revolving in the sharpish breeze –
Sharpish for June –
He smiles that Dublin Bay smile of his.

He cries: "O worms of Sandymount Strand!
Declare to God your Credit Card expiry dates!
Do you know any other city in the world
With not merely a seashore
On the sillstone of its inner city
But a muddy seashore
And all of that lone and level mud
Shelling its own eggs,
Peels of worms?
Where be your pink buckets?
Where be your pink spades?
Where be your pink inflatable wings?"

Maria Teresa is in heaven number eleven
Dangling on every spondee of the poet Mahon.
She is not swooping back to Rio de Janeiro
Until tomorrow night
But already she has had her weekend
Epitomized by the poet Mahon.
He bows out. We walk on
Talking about him in front of his back.
Literally – just as he would wish it.

Fame
Is having all Ireland
Talking about you
In front of your back.

Dusk, two empty teacups;
A meagre, white man kneeling
At the knees of an ample, black woman;
Two worms expanding on the floor;
Writhing in the mud,
Crying out –
But in cyclonic silence –
For the ceremonial knives
Of each other's afterlives.

A knock on the window.
More a tap than a knock.
A courier?
At this hour?

My nextdoor neighbour wanting to know
If I would be kind enough to move my car.
I'm sorry – I can't move my car:
I'm with a Mahon scholar on the floor.

Lighting up time in the back streets of Dublin:
At the twitch, the streetlights of pink, fizzy sodium.
My visitor from Rio de Janeiro
Crawling up the window,
Saluting the silhouette –
Equestrian chimera in cloudsea –
Of her sailor-under-the-horizon hero,
Her island-in-the-rain maestro, Captain Mahon.

Brazilian Footballer – Please Do Not Pedestalize

He came to me with a blue raincoat and an introduction;
He was bashfully boyish, jaw-crushingly shy.
But when he was leaving he could not find his blue raincoat.
For almost an hour I had to turn my place
Upside down searching for his blue raincoat
While my friends kept their eyes shut listening to Chico
  Buarque.
"This is so bizarre" he kept repeating "this is so bizarre".
In the end, of course, we did find his blue raincoat.
It was rolled up inside his green, yellow and blue kitbag.
When he'd gone I breathed a brazen sigh of relief
Only a half-hour later to hear my brass knocker crashing
And my doorbell detonating in its brass plate.
It was him back again solemnly seeking
His red-and-white Top Flight umbrella – solemnly! –
As if somehow it was I who had kidnapped
His blue raincoat and his red-and-white Top Flight umbrella.
He vanished out into the night, like a virgin into a swoon:
Brazilian Footballer – Please Do Not Pedestalize.

North Inner City Brazilian Monkey

My God, let this chalice never pass from me.

A warm, wet, June evening in the North Inner City;
A Georgian terrace on the Royal Canal;
The ultramodern East Stand of Croke Park swirling above me;
I am hovering on granite steps waiting for a door to open.

In five minds thinking: is that a monkey in a cage?
And, if it is, is it a Brazilian monkey?
No bird of these bombed-out parts makes a like complaint.
If it is a mating whistle, what a hurting whistle!

The cage is part-concealed the far side of the canal;
A black metal platform on a black metal pole;
I think I can descry a mesh of wire;
Red on black stripes of a Brazilian monkey akimbo.

The door opens and above me smiling
Sways a tall, red-headed woman in a black ballgown.
I lose my feet and stagger backwards down the steps.
"You found me all right?" she whispers "You found me
    all right?"

In the ante-room to her bedroom she hands me
Her bow and arrow she brought back from Manaus in
    Amazonia;
I hold the bow in my hands, appreciating the weight of it;
She whispers that she herself hails from the Glen of Aherlow.

My God, let this chalice never pass from me.

The Chicago Waterstone's

I'm your girlfriend from the past
And I'm always thinking of you.

When you're revisiting her city
On your twenty-two-city reading tour to promote
Your latest, barcoded,
Extracted-with-great lethargy
Volume which your ingenious publicists advertise as
"The most accessible poetry
Since Mallarmé"
She leaves a message at your hotel,
The Chicago Ramada.
With your mouth in your heart
You make haste to phone her
Only to get her answer machine:
Her voice is throatier, darker,
More intimate, yet more formal than before.
She commands you to leave a message after the tone.

Next day you meet her in the restaurant
Of the Art Institute of Chicago
And after you have ejaculated –
Excessively as always –
Over Caillebotte's
Rainy Day, Paris
She tells you how marvellous you look –
That you haven't changed in ten years
In spite of your grey hair and bifocal lenses.
For five seconds you believe her.
She drops names like a rabbit on a rampage:
"Saw Simmons last week in NY. How's Carson?"

43

She condescends to refer to your new book
As if you were a neurotic travelling salesman
Which in fact of course is what you are.
She simply yearns to know about its title
A Snail in My Prime:
"I simply yearn to know
Why did you call it
A Snail in My Prime?
Does it allude to an artwork?
Perhaps a *hommage* to Matisse?"
She yodels: "It resonates with allusion."
She enquires about the reading tonight
In the Chicago Waterstone's.
Brandishing her eyelashes
And pulling down tight
Her Greenpeace T-shirt
Over her Anti-Global Warming breasts
She enthuses: "I will be there."

But when you're getting up to go
And you're kissing her on both cheeks
Just a little bit too fervently
She confides that she's not a hundred per cent sure
If she can actually make it tonight
"Because of a priority engagement
And you know what priority engagements are like,
I guess."

I do. I guess I do.
In the Spring of 1985
When I was the Robert Frost Fellow
In Franconia, New Hampshire
And she was my Monitor
And I was sitting out on the porch
Doing my best to do nothing

As prescribed by the master,
The Old Silk Worm Frost,
Scanning Mount Lafayette,
The Notch beyond the maples,
The Dragon in the Fog,
She whispered acoustically
Like an Arabist
Deciphering the Koran
"You have such – such
Goddamn-turquoise eyes"
And as I blushed like a baboon –
Like a baboon's bottom –
Gravely she enquired
"May I comb your pony tail?"
And while I dilly-dallied
She plopped her anchor
Into my shallow waters,
Her chic, little, five-clawed, Tiffany's grapnel.

At the reading in the Chicago Waterstone's
There is not a sign of her.
You scan the empty chairs.
Every time the door behind you opens
You glance around. It dawns
On you what she had in mind
And there is nothing you can do but wince,
Wince through the reading,
Wince back to the hotel,
Sit up in bed late into the night wincing;
Draining your bladder;
The Chicago Waterstone's;
Draining your bladder;
The Robert Frost Silk Farm;
Draining your bladder;
At the airport in the morning wince;

At O'Hare wince;
Wince & wince & wince & wince & wince & wince;
Wincing all the way back to Shannon;
Wincing in Shannon in the dark before the dawn;
Wincing into Dublin in the rain at 7.30 a.m.;
Wincing in the Long Term Carpark;
Wincing all the way back the road to Slane
To the home of your 1995 girlfriend
Who looks up from her book *Wild Swans*
And says "Oh – it's you."

I'm your girlfriend from the past
And I'm always thinking of you.

Remote Control

In the summer of '97 I lost my Remote Control
And it ruined the summer and all belonging to me.

I reported to the woman at the counter of Multichannel.
She looked so severe I was slow to speak to her.
I stammered: "I have – I have lost my Remote Control."

She, all her bones like fish undulating underwater,
Her eyes swooping like kites,
Her breasts kicking up dust under her blue blouse,

She replied: "I can find you a Remote Control."
I said: "But it's lashing rain outside."
She flung up the counter hatch amd strode out in a red
　　pelmet mini,

All thirty-odd years of her, with a striped golfing umbrella.
She strode out into the streets of Drogheda
Where the River Boyne had already burst its banks.

She strode across the flooded street – the mud
Flecking her white legs with black sequins,
Her high heels pricking the puddles.

She jumped into a white '97 Seat Ibiza and signalled
For me to jump in beside her.
She drove up the town and into the Lourdes Hospital.

"There is a man up here with a Remote Control like yours
But he doesn't need it anymore."
She flew into the hospital under the feathers of her stripes.

Back down at the counter of Multichannel
I signed a receipt for the dead man's Remote Control.
I asked her: "Was it cancer?"

"Yes" – she sighed – "it was cancer, cancer of the bowel.
Cancer is all over the shop.
I think you will have more luck with his Remote Control."

I have had a lot more luck with his Remote Control.
Dr Dillon says he's never seen me looking so well:
"What any man needs is a good woman and buckets of television."

Yes, and the way it is now on bright, warm, September mornings
Before even I get out of bed the television
In the corner of my bedroom is beseeching to be switched on

Especially on Saturday mornings at 9 a.m.;
Channel 4's morning racing preview;
John McCririck in Big Top form: tick-tack; good going.

A good woman is a Jewish jeweller.
Beyond words are good women
Bejewelling telephone lines.

Never before has it felt so good to be alive
Thanks to the woman at the counter of Multichannel;
Her politics, her technique, her take it-or-leave-it audacity.

*In the autumn of '97 I was gifted another man's Remote Control
And it made my autumn, and all belonging to me.*

O God! O Dublin!

Ottawa – on my last day –
I had lunch in a café downtown,
Memories on Clarence.
Al fresco on the terrace.
Gaspacho, tuna.

When I went to read the check
The server –
A woman, black –
Had scrawled across it in red biro:
"I love you."
I read it again:
"I love you."

I went inside back of Memories;
Indicated an anxiousness with my eyebrows
To have a word in the ear of the server.
I asked her: "What did you write that for?"
She shrugged, baring
Her double-ditch of white teeth:
"I love lots."

I said: "But . . ."
"No buts . . ." she snapped

'I loved you the very minute you sat down'.
I said: 'What is your name?'
She said: "Lily – Lily McManus."
"Where are you from, Lily?"

"I was born in Ethiopia
 But I married an Irishman."
"Oh God, Lily! I was born in Ireland
 But I didn't marry an Ethiopian."

On the plane trip back home to Dublin
I had time to ask myself many questions.
Many many many many many questions.
Why did I marry an Irishwoman?
God knows in Dublin in 1967
Ethiopians were not thick on the ground.

Everything that could go wrong on a plane trip
Did go wrong: the nose
Had to be replaced with a spare nose;
We had to divert to Montreal;
We had to stack over Heathrow;
At the carousel in Dublin
My Samsonite overnighter failed to materialize.

I turned up at my brother-in-law's bagless.
I asked my brother-in-law who was digging
Holes in the front garden:
"Why do Irish marry Irish?
Wouldn't you think that Irish
Would have more bottle in their water?"
My brother-in-law brandished his spade
In his two hands and grinned
A big, five-faced, close-up grin:
"Durcan, if you say another word,
I'll top you."

But, Lily,
It is even worse than that.
Not only do Limericks marry Limericks,

Corks Corks,
Downs Downs,
Offalys Offalys,
But Ringsenders marry Ringsenders,
Ballsbridgers Ballsbridgers,
Sandymounters Sandymounters!

Ethiopia, would you not give Ottawa to marry me?
O God! O Dublin!

Dirty Day Derry

When I ask the young widow for a cylinder of gas
She laughs: " Have you chained up your empty?"
She loves to be able to say that to me.
"Have you chained up your empty?"

As outside in the street in the storm
In which people are crouching to keep on their feet
And umbrellas are lying dead in the gutter
Turned inside out –

Although the young widow's heart lies a-bleeding,
She folds her arms under her bust and peers out
The window over the stacked cornflakes laughing at me –
An older man chaining up his empty.

I know all about boys and girls:
About gas, about chains, about empties.

Norway

Only in Norway were his talents adequately recognized.
Guardian, 13 November 1997

At the request of the Assistant Director
I consented to have my head carved
For the permanent collection
Of the National Gallery in Universitetsgaten.

At 12.15 p.m. on a lurid July day in Oslo
I knocked on the stonecarver's door
Waiting for the big, raw, high-cheeked, side-whiskered
Stonecarver to fling it open and roar at me lustily.

A short, slender woman in green anorak,
Blue jeans, black boots,
Curls down to her waist,
Peeked out the door, curtseyed.

Not speaking, she led me down a dark passage
Into a large, high-ceilinged room
Overlooking an overgrown garden
With a disused bath, an old sycamore,
A clothesline pegged with men's shirts
And whose walls were not spiked.

She spoke: Please sit up on the stool.
It was a high stool which sprung up and down
As well as spinning around.
She stood concealed behind a block of limestone.
She started chiselling, hammering.

Her brisk companionableness,
Her intellectual candour,
Above all her courtesy –
All those things in a good woman
For which over
His several lifetimes
An innocent man pines.

After the second sitting
I could not bear to go back to her
But of course I had to.
In between threaded, winding anecdotes
About her esteemed husband –
He works in Information Technology, she enlightened me –
Or about photographers and sculptors
She had known in Trondheim and Narvik –
I knew each of them so very well, she confided –
She'd make observations
Of a precise nature
About my – as she called them – features.
What is your mouth made of?
Where are those eyes of yours?
Are your nostrils real?
Are your eyebrows your own?
Your nose is all of you.
I want more of your neck.

One afternoon when the sky was reddening up
And I was thinking of saying to her –
Look, I am afraid I cannot come anymore –
She announced: *I don't need you anymore.*

Those were her exact words:
I don't need you anymore.
Can you conceive of being a man

Wanting to be silent –
To be silent forever –
With this one particular woman in Norway
And with no other woman in the cosmos
And she says ever so punctiliously
I don't need you anymore?

Five days ago.
I am still in bed.
Can't think. Can't eat.
To end up in a tiny white room
On my back in Oslo
With my hand on bone;
Not on *her* bone;
On *my* bone;
Not being able to get out of bed
After having had my head carved
By a married woman stonecarver in Norway.

I don't need you anymore.

Eriugena

I went out to the Hazel Wood
Because I had been invited
To a party out there –
Manus and Lyn, drinks, 12 to 2.
Went early, left early.
Found myself standing
Alone in the Hazel Wood
At the bottom of which
In the gateway
Stood a woman of whom
I have been always nervous
Because she is the silentest
Woman in Valleymount.
I lurked behind a tree
Waiting for her to drive off
In her Nissan Bluebird.

But she was not driving off.
She was exercising a vast Irish
Wolfhound dog – a sort of shaggy polar bear.
I am not ashamed to admit that I am scared
Of vast Irish Wolfhound dogs.
Nevertheless I came out of hiding.
A north wind blew and dusk
Was closing in on Valleymount.
I strolled down into the gateway
Pretending not to have a care in the world.

Without looking at me – rather gazing up
Into the Hazel Wood through tinted hornrimmed spectacles –

As if calling out the name of her lover –
She called out the name of her wolfhound and again:
Eriugena! Eriugena!
He was stumbling about the Hazel Wood from tree to tree –
A massive ripple of tenderness in search of a shore.
Eriugena! Eriugena!
She had the voice of a woman about to commit suicide
On the spear of her lover.
Eriugena! Eriugena!

I said: As in Philosopher on Banknote?
She answered: As in Philosopher on Banknote.
As I drove off I waved to her
But she did not return my wave.
In my rear view mirror
I watched her embrace her wolfhound,
Licking him on the throat,
The pair of them soaring up on their hind quarters
As one female centaur silhouetted in winter
On the shores of the Black Sea.
God the Daughter!

3 JANUARY 1994

O'Donnell Abu!

I like to lock myself into the toilet,
To sit on the bowl
And to leaf through my teenage daughter's
Copy of *Green* magazine:
"Why Do Robins Have Red Breasts?"
On the floor at my feet
Her *Book of Five Hundred Questions*:
"How many legs has a giraffe?"

My husband does not approve of me
Reading in the lavatory.
Yet he is always wanting us to make love
On the drawing-room floor.
He insists I put newspapers on the floor
But woe betide me
If I put the wrong newspaper on the floor.
When he rears up like a horse
Shying at a triple fence
And collapses between my knees
He is as likely to say "Don't tell me
You put today's *Irish Times* on the floor"
As "You're more delicious than Audrey Hepburn."

I have a friend in Malaga who is dying
Of cancer. But she never says so.
She says: "I am still sitting on the bowl."
Or: "I have not yet fallen off the bowl."
Lord, when my turn comes to fall
Off the bowl, let me fall

All in one tumble, one swoop
– Like a giraffe – like a robin redbreast –
With my feet up in the air.
O'Donnell Abu!

Death of a Dorkel

I

I am the son of Simon Snorkel
Singing for my supper –
A silver salver of snowy strawberries.
On a Sunday in summer in Spain
I am scooped by the spectacle of a señora
Serenading me with her solitude;
Seldom have I seen such savagery
And such softness in the same señora,
Such a snip of sleep.

II

I drive back down into the Alhambra
With in my boot only fiction,
Not a pinch of Sunday newspaper;
Remembering not only kisses
But her praises of what she terms
My economical use of devices.
At last at fifty in the sun
Given death to by a woman;
I am a Dorkel.

III

I am the son of Simon Snorkel
Singing for my supper –
A silver salver of snowy strawberries.
On a Sunday in summer in Spain

I am scooped by the spectacle of a señora
Serenading me with her solitude;
Seldom have I seen such savagery
And such softness in the same señora,
Such a snip of sleep.

IV

A Dorkel who cares only for the moment
But who *for* that moment and *in* that moment
Is courteous, devoted, tender
To her every minifreckle, her every minimole;
To her every soliloquy, to her every pause.
Only in the small print of her script
Do I come alive wholly and I decline
To be sad at losing her so finally –
My God Almighty lady.

V

I am the son of Simon Snorkel
Singing for my supper –
A silver salver of snowy strawberries.
On a Sunday in summer in Spain
I am scooped by the spectacle of a señora
Serenading me with her solitude;
Seldom have I seen such savagery
And such softness in the same señora,
Such a snip of sleep.

The Binman Cometh

to Michael Kane

I

To be a Binman
You have to love your native place.
A journalist can skirt around patriotism
But for a Binman there can be no skirting around.
A Binman has to put his hands where his mouth is.

II

A Binman's business
Is – with his hands –
To look at things.
My father brought me up to look *on*;
His father brought him up to look *back*;
Now I'm bringing up my own son to look *up*.
My hands are my eyes.
My hands see into every corner of Ballsbridge,
Every lilac nook,
Every saffron cranny:
From the bandstand in Herbert Park
Down to the Liffey Skyline;
From the Kiosk on Pembroke Road
Down to the Gasometer on the Docks.

III

Being a Binman is a vocation.
Even on my day off

Other people think of me as being
The Binman.

IV

I drive a car – which other people find odd.
They do not expect to see the Binman driving a car.
Well, I do. I drive a car the colour of which
Has never been seen on this earth before –
A blacker shade of pink –
But my neighbour Miss Fleming likes it.
She stands in the doorway of her one up and one down
In her blue nightie and with a red towel
On her head and she drools –
Oh I do like the colour of your car!

I drive down to the coast of Ballsbridge
Where the sea meets up with the reclaimed land.
I am not averse to having a dip.
I like the feel of my bare breasts.
Once I saw a Government Minister in the nip
But I'd nicer breasts than he had.
I'm proud of my nipples –
My nipples could jump over a Government Minister.
He had big, flat, lumpy, hairy, nippleless knobs of yokes.

I drive home to the old lady.
We take it in turns
To divert one another.
Tonight, she whispers, she's a guitar.
She invites me to play her,
A slow air,
A bit of strumming,
Then a big flamenco
In which I am the bull,

63

She is the matador.
Neither of us ever knows
When, where, how
It will end
Except in darkness –
Golden darkness
With seed on the sheets,
With blood on the sand;
Buckets of blood,
Buckets of seed.
Have you got a tissue, dear?
Toilet roll will do.

I quiz her in the dark:
Do you love me?
She splutters:
What do you mean do I love you?
What would I be doing
Hanging out of you
Like a rat
At the top of my bed
If I didn't love you?

First thing next morning –
Seagulls screeching at our window
Frantic to dive into our bin –
She'll yawn at me:
Pounce down to the Kiosk and catch me a newspaper.
She's addicted to newspapers – I never read them.
I am the Binman – garbage is my life.

Island Musician Going Home

after Veronica Bolay

Driving home alone the bog road at night in the rain
Leaving the village behind me, its harbour lights
Pegging down the marquee of the sea,
I am half sunk by the stone of my heart.

Mile after mile of bog road in the night in the rain,
Not a single dwelling on the mountain either side of the road,
Not knowing when a mountain sheep will light up under my
    wheels,
My audience all couples canoodling behind in the village.

But when I drive up to my maroon-painted five-barred gate
And switch off my lights, and climb out of my car,
And I can see nothing, and I can hear nothing,
I see again that home is the skirl of silence.

I kiss the darkness, and all loneliness abandons me.
A life without a wife is nothing to boast about
But that's music. I walk back up the road
Kissing the darkness; and a small mouth of cold gold

In the clouds is becoming aware of its soul.

The Bellewstown Waltz

To think that once I was a mahatma
Who used wear a pajama!

Elongating myself here in the nip between clean sheets
On a summer's night, waiting for *you!*

Cremated ashes steaming past on crenellated waters:
Oh God's Breath!

You are having a bath.
In your own Sanskrit, "having a soak".

Gurgle stop gurgle stop gurgle gurgle
Stop gurgle gurgle stop gurgle stop

Your technique of letting the water out in installments,
Manipulating the plug with your two big toes.

(Your two big toes! I will never get
Within a nail paring of that big-toe-to-big-toe intimacy!)

I close my eyes, inhale the cotton sheets,
The breeze in the cotton.

Only this afternoon I hung them out to dry;
They dried in less than an hour.

I took them in, folded them on my own,
Carried them upstairs in my arms, made the bed.

You are towelling down. Slash hooks of silence.
Your bare feet on the back stairs.

Your goosepimple knees dripping onto bare boards.
"Which nightdress shall I wear?"

You enquire rhetorically from the doorway
Before diving in at the deep end

Of the pillow-garlanded, raft-and-altar bed.
Counting me

When you bite on my ear:
"And one-two-three . . . one-two-three . . ."

Instructing me not
To forget to bring you your tea

In the purple-stained porcelain teapot.
"And one-two-three . . . one-two-three . . ."

Lyons Gold Label?
No, no, no, no.

"And one-two-three . . ."
Keemun?

Keemun!
"And one-two-three. . . one-two-three . . ."

I didn't know you knew how to waltz.
Snail, shut your shell!

The Bellewstown Waltz!
The Beautiful Bellewstown Waltz!

Thistles

Middle-aged lovers –
Gossips brand us.
We blush.
How I wish
We could have had children of our own!

Instead the field outside our bedroom window
Is a roofless crèche of thistles:
A homeless thistle for every child we might have had;
A tatoo of embryos
Whose fingernails have never been cut.

As we grow older
We make love more easily –
Polythenely, polythenely –
Throwing caution to the nitpickers at the gates
And to the crawthumpers in their charabancs.
I teach you Chinese boxing.
You teach me Thai.
You arm wrestle me and, as always, win.

Kicking up clouds of thistledown,
Washed up on our pillows,
Circled round
By seven or eight vases of sweet pea,
We glimpse the winds reap
The practical consequences of our spirit combat –
The prickly, theoretical ghosts of our might-have-been children.

II

Lopes
Our hardy neighbour
Old Farmer God
With ashplant stick
Slashing the skulls off our thistles.
In the wake of his wellington boots
Transports of headless urchins
Skulk in our field
With their tiny, green, boney fists twined
In polythene bouquets
In front of their big, bloated, empty bellies
Beseeching us for a life we cannot give to them.

Dearest, when you catch me by surprise tonight
At a corner of twilight;
When you step out from behind a screen of dusk
Between bathroom and bedroom;
When between window shutter and wardrobe mirror
You take the pins out of your hair;
When at your dressing table
You pluck out your spikey earrings;
When on top of your chest of drawers
You lay out your amethyst rings;
When on your floor
You throw down your keys
And step out of your skirt,
Your wrap-around skirt;
When from the hook on the back of the door
You hoist on one hand
Your white silk nightdress;
While our ghost progeny hold their breath;

I am going to ask you to dance with me
Upside down on the Ceiling of Old Age –
On the Floor of First Infancy.

IV

When Old Farmer God asks me
"Do you not know
That thistles are an offence?"
I am going to stand on my head
And wreath my feet around your neck
And wait for your fingers to nip
Down my shinbones into my thighs
And there will be a silence
In which we will hear only
Ourselves crying out one another's names
And the actual grinding of the original sugar cane
And the juice spewing down the chute
And a rush of thistledown accumulating
To percolate out down across the field
And the clatter of its seed seeding itself,
All that genetic *tohu-bohu*,
All that pedigree *ruaille buaille*,
All that metaphysical *brouhaha*.

We will go down into sleep –
Be it in war or peace –
To a sitting-down-from-hunger ovation
From our might-have-been children:
Their keen-eyed, gratuituous, omniscient, exhausted applause.

October Break (Lovers)

She and I are sitting out in the conservatory
Of the Renvyle House Hotel in Connemara,
Recommended to me by John McGahern,
On a bright October afternoon, rain
Milking down on the glass roof.
After the waitress has brought us out
A tray of coffee and scones and jam,
Laid it down on the glasstopped wickerwork table,
She sits back down into her wickerwork chair with her book,
A large volume in a red dustjacket
With a reproduction of Klimt's "The Kiss":
The World Treasury of Love Stories
Selected and Introduced by Lucy Rosenthal
With a Foreword by Clifton Fadiman.

II

I sit back in my wickerwork chair and stare up
At the redistribution of raindrops on the glass roof,
At her two eyes redistributing the words of love stories.
For seven years I have been her lover.
For seven years visiting her in her home.
For seven years coming and going.

III

Wandering around Ireland at the height of summer
I visited John McGahern and his wife Madeleine

74

In their County Leitrim home
On the shores of Laura Lake.
He told me about the American woman
Who had fallen in love and bought a home.
He took me in his car and drove up the side of a mountain,
The Iron Mountain.
On top of the mountain he got out,
Leapt across a stream
Loose with yellow loosestrife,
Disappeared off into a clump of trees,
High sycamores round a litter of stones.
He declared: "Well, now, isn't this a grand place!"

IV

She closes her book and smiles and I say
"Do you mind me asking you a question?"
And she says "Not at all" and I say
"Is it possible for a lover to have a home?"
And she says "Unfortunately not" and I say "Why?"
And she says "We don't have children of our own"
And I say "What does that mean?"
And she says "Home is where children are"
And she smiles and I smile and we stare
In silence at the glass walls all around us
Beseiged by precipitation
And I estimate that over the last seven years
She and I must have made love one or two
Thousand times and where have all *those* children gone?
Where have all those *raindrops* run off to?
Where is *their* home?
Our home?
I enquire: "Is it a good book?"

She exclaims: "It is the ideal book":
The World Treasury of Love Stories
Selected and Introduced by Lucy Rosenthal
With a Foreword by Clifton Fadiman.

Flying Over the Kamloops

Out strolling the towpath of the River Blackwater
On the last Sunday afternoon in October
The sons of her first marriage
Make way for us to stroll on ahead of them
And we fall to talking about death and legacies.
She announces: "Of course I will leave everything to
    my sons."
I ask: "But what about me?"

We glance abruptly at one another
Before both looking away.
Neither of us knows what to say.
I say: "What's that?"
She says "Do you mean the watercress
Or the hart's tongue fern?"

The sons of her first marriage –
Grown-up men taller than I am –
Catch up with us and they weave
A small circle inside of which
For her and them to walk.

I try to keep up with them,
Tripping along outside their circlet.
She is telling them
How the day before yesterday –
While I was staring out at the night
From the jet en route to London from Vancouver –
Her dog ate a squirrel live
And how, far from being sad, she was glad

With her dog's commitment to dogginess.
She admired the alacrity
With which her dog devoured the squirrel live.

She is laughing solemnly
And the sons of her first marriage
Concelebrate in her laughter
And she looks over at me,
Peers out quizically
From within her circlet at me,
And I peer into the river –
Night flowing east to the sun –
And I hear the man sitting next to me in the jet murmur:
"I am flying home because my mother is getting married."
I stand still, staring into the river.
I look him in the eyes:
"Where are we now?"
"Flying over the Kamloops."
He is quite certain:
"Flying over the Kamloops."

Man Circling His Woman's Sundial

On a July evening in my fifty-second year –
My woman has gone to Greece on a cruise
With the Women's Democratic Association –
I drink a bottle of white wine and I get
To feeling better about the world and I put
A CD into the CD player and I sit
In the front room of her farm house
On the couch with its back to the window –
The trim, hard couch she got newly upholstered
After I'd retrieved it from my first wife's skip –
My first wife acquired it twenty-five years ago
From the Booles who were dumping it –
The Booles later also split up –
Is there a marriage in Ireland
That has not split up? –
Is Joe Lee in Cork
The only man in Ireland
Still in the married state?
Still saying "I do"? –
I recline with my right arm idling
Along the rim of the back, listening
To Tom Waits – "Innocent When You Dream" –
And the sunlight is sliding in the window
And all the years that have gone past –
That I had thought were dispersed for ever –
Are regrouping down in the glens of the carpet
Like the clans of the MacGregors
And it is the case that nothing that I have done –
Not the least thing, good or bad, is expiring;
Everything is alive, gilt-edged, piping.

*

In the big mirror over the white marble mantelpiece
I can see the reflection of her sundial on the lawn.
Halfway down the bottle of white wine I get a brainwave:
I will phone the parish priest and ask him
If when I die he would kindly arrange
For my ashes to be buried under my woman's sundial.
I pick up the phone and I dial the parish priest's number.
He whispers: "Is this the drink talking, Paul?"
"No, Father, it is me – the real me."
He is sympathetic, solicitous, soulful – sisterly even.
Bishop Smith, he insists, will be supportive.
When men are sisterly, there is truth in the valley.

I gaze out the window at her garden
On which she has worked all her life and I see
My woman's reflection in the window.
Possessive, yes; aloof, even – but so what?
With her silver goose-topped walking stick
She is at peace with Greece.

After two thousand acts of love,
Hurt, negligence, thoughtlessness,
We still bear affection for one another.
Tonight everything is coming together –
Coming together and falling apart,
Falling apart and coming together –
Delphinium, iris, opium poppy, mullein,
Seagull rose, yellow loosestrife, sumac;
I am two hours behind her;
She is two hours ahead of me;
My woman in Greece pole-vaulting at nightfall
The cracks between the flagstones of Doric temples.

Next morning I wake with a shock to recall
That I phoned the parish priest and said what I said.

Maybe it is time to give up the wine
Or – at my age – to stick to the herbal tea.
Yet when I walk out into her garden
And walk around her sundial and finger it,
Decipher it, stand by it, go by it,
I rejoice that I asked him to bury my ashes under it
For this is what more than anything else in the world
I want – to rest in peace under my woman's sundial.
Life is a deathwish – an open secret
To share and rejoice in and not to be ashamed of.
Only then will my woman wholly appreciate me –
In the finale of my corruption –
Wholly comprehend the body she has lain with
Two thousand times in the dark in the magnolia white
        bedroom.

I turn and behold again in the drawing-room window
My woman smiling in at me –
My tiny-footed broad-shouldered Chinese
Feudal swordswoman smiling down at me.
I am dead – wonderfully dead – and I am gazing up
Into her all-merciful eyes.

High in the Cooley

I wanted to publish a poem
That would include the word "fuck"
Not as a gimmick
But as the jewel in the crown

Of the vocabulary of affection.
Soon as you utter the word "fuck"
Gusts of divinity suck
At the breasts of erosion.

I wanted to celebrate my luck
At having made with my woman a home
High in the Cooley by composing a poem
With at its vortex the word "fuck".

I wanted to christen the poem
"Teilhard de Chardin"
Or "The Phenomenon of Woman" or "Mass
Upon the Altar of the Universe".

It was useless. They were afraid to publish.
Editors not knowing their own water.
Parishioners ashamed of their own parish.
Cosmopolitans ashamed of their own cosmos.

Thirty years later I drive home
To read to my woman alone
My "Phenomenon of Woman" poem:
"We wanted to fuck in the ocean".

By fireside two otters
Undress; on parquet roll.
Old otters squeaking soul:
All that matters.

The Only Isaiah Berlin
of the Western World

The first adult book I read was by Isaiah Berlin
When I was fourteen;
On my mother's ticket for Switzer's Lending Library
In Grafton Street
I borrowed *Karl Marx* by Isaiah Berlin.
It was the author's name more than the title
That seduced me.
Karl Marx was taboo-illicit
But Isaiah Berlin was omnipotent-prophetic.

Omnipotent-prophetic
With in my arms Isaiah Berlin
I cycled home
With no hands on the handlebars
To 57 Dartmouth Square
On the banks of the Grand Canal
Knowing in the backs of my legs
I was cycling into the Russia of my fate;
A motorcycle escort of the years
All around me at the bridge
In a thirty-strong ring of outriders;
Into the Russia of my tiny fate
To knock knees with Isaiah Berlin
On the banks of the Fontanka.

It was October in Leningrad –
Golden canalbanks, true love, mortality;
Armenian women, Afghan colonels;
Diarrhoea, herbal tea.

Isaiah Berlin took me under his wing:
Skipping sessions
We walked the canals conferring, conferring;
We walked the summer gardens conferring, conferring;
Pushkin, Gogol, Turgenev, Herzen.
By banks of red primula candelabra
He stooped tall and taught me:
"No end can justify the means.
The evilest murder is the political murder."
I glanced down through mottled, veined freckles
Into the big, broad hands of his enthusiasm.
I said: "Poetry is pure research." He clapped hands and sang.
I said: "I am a Protestant Tinker!" He bassooned:
    "Double Odium!"

On Apothecary Street
He bent down and picked up a leaf –
A lime-tree leaf, I think it was –
And he handed it to me
As if it was the most precious, rarest, yellow rose in the world;
The yellow rose
Which is the flower of friendship.

I knew then that my soul
Was a young girl who was born
And should never die –
A princess, proud, unhappy, unappeasable –
And that is how I have lived my life;
Either floating in my own immortality
Or getting punched in the eyes
By a bewhiskered auctioneer
Who fears and loathes me
Because I write poetry and love love;
Who derides me
"Nobody could live with the likes of you."

Isaiah Berlins don't grow on trees
And now I have lost him,
I have lost him surely –
The only Isaiah Berlin of the Western World.

17 NOVEMBER 1997

Karamazov in Ringsend

In our redbrick terrace – a cul-de-sac in Ringsend –
Everybody parks their car tight to the kerb.
Not least the poet Durcan. Watch him
As he drives up and slides backwards
Into his space in front of his front door
Which hasn't seen a lick of paint in thirteen years,
All cracks, blisters, stains, smears.
Sometimes he spends up to ten minutes
Parking – getting tight to the kerb,
Slotting into his sacred parenthesis of five-and-a-half metres.

Next door to him – three houses down –
Resides the politician Mary Banotti.
The way she parks her car
Demonstrates not only the difference
Between the solemn poet and the carefree politician
But the difference between a man and a woman.
She drives up at speed and she leaps out
Almost before she has stopped, leaving her car
At least six inches from the kerb,
Sometimes even more than a whole twelve inches,
Her front wheels locked to outward and away.

When the pair of them have disappeared
In behind their separate doors
And the small, sprightly, bedenimed figure
Of Karamazov in Ringsend
Materializes out of snow
Searching for his Mokroe

It is Mary Banotti's door and keyhole
That he presses against, lends an ear to,
Before whirling around and hullabalooing like a blue-flamed
    house alarm:
Whip up the horses, Andrei, and drive up with a dash!

Behind the man poet's door he can hear only the groans of
    the drowned;
Behind the woman politician's door he can hear only the
    laughter of the saved.

Notes Towards a Necessary Suicide

The practical consequences of loneliness and depression –
Apart from a tendency to contemplate suicide at awkward
    moments –
Meeting an acquaintance on the street and having to rock
Back on my heels in affability –
Are taking an age to do the washing up
Or taking another age to make the bed
Or, in both cases, winding up by doing neither
Or, as was the case this morning,
In a tactic to buck the rut,
Driving over to Sandymount Strand,
Only to find myself unable to get out of the car.

I sit up in the driving seat
Trying to keep sitting upright,
Trying not to put my head in my hands,
Trying to concentrate on Dublin Bay's gallops of white horses.
I drive back to my den, fretful
I might not be able to make it
From cardoor to housedoor,
I climb up the stair – climb and climb and climb
And climb and climb
And climb and climb and climb –
And get into bed in my clothes
And pulverize the ceiling
With making-eyes blinks
Before pulling down a pillow over my head
And listening to the booming of my own sobbing.

Ad infinitum I think of Virginia Woolf and know
That sooner or later I will have to go down to the river:
The Dodder at night where it flows past Lansdowne Rugby
    Ground
And join my father and his brothers down among the
    umbrellas and fridges,
The hoops and the horseshoes.
I have always been affiliated to umbrellas and fridges,
Hoops and horseshoes.
I think of buckets of champagne and rain bucketing down.
Not perish but relish the prospect of suicide
In the rain with ice-cold champagne.

"In Ringsend Park this morning the body was discovered
Of the middle-aged, minor-major poet Paul Durcan
In black suit, white shirt, bow tie
Under a tree in the rain with piles
Of empty champagne bottles all around him,
Greeting cards, faxes, bouquets.
His amused colleagues did not express astonishment;
All were agreed that he was,
In the words of Brian Ryan, playwright,
"A serious man for the weddings."

Mecca

Walking at evening in Saudi Arabia
On the outskirts of Mecca,
On the shores of the reservoir,
In tropical suit, collar and tie,
I am startled to see pull up ahead of me
A white car with amber beacons on its roof,
An array of black aerials,
Blue words on its door panels in English and Arabic –
Highway Patrol.
The moment of truth I have been dreading all my life.
Although I am guilty of nothing, I fill up with guilt.

A small, dark, lean man jumps out of the driving seat.
He is wearing neither keffiyah nor jellaba
But an undersuit of blue jeans and white blouse.
He cries: Stop – are you Irish poet?
I admit I am Irish poet. He cries:
We are International Security – Highway Patrol.
Our obligation is to protect king's swordsman
Who tomorrow has one beheading on plate.
We like to have your Visa Card number and Expiry Date.

A small, squat, ladylike gentleman climbs out
Of the back seat of the car and proffers a gilt-edged
Notebook with a Ball Pentel pen. He indicates –
With a curved gesture of his left arm –
He would like me to stand the far side of the car
Out of sight of the young men in the nearby tent.
He murmurs – staring out at the middle of the reservoir –
"This is good place to commit suicide."

94

The driver, standing the other side of me,
Puts his hand on my shoulder.
"What we do, like to do,
Is to reflate inflatable dummy,
Tow out into reservoir, deflate.
It is finished, over, kaput, accounted for.
Meantime we have one beheading on plate.
Thank you for your co-operation. Please always
Remember that you are in Mecca. Goodnight."

Holy Smoke

The problem of being a poet
Is the problem of being always right.

Irish Subversive

This morning when I woke up it dawned on me
That yesterday was not a nightmare;
That what happened at Bristol Airport Security
Actually did happen.

The previous day I'd been
Touch judge
For the Cardiff–Biarritz match
At the Arms Park.

Not a match to remember;
The French were tetchy.
The French are always tetchy
On away grounds.

Yesterday morning at the check-in
At Bristol International Airport
Who should I meet but Paul Durcan,
The bloody poet.

I'd never met him before
But my sister and his sister
Were in the same class together
In the Sacred Heart Convent in Leeson Street
Forty years ago.
So I introduced myself. To my astonishment
He was able to place me immediately.
Phenomenal memory these poet chaps have.

After checking-in together we sauntered
Along the departure tunnel
Towards the security chap at his checkpoint.
He enquired of Durcan
What was his occupation.
With the ferocious intensity of a man
Facing immediate execution
By firing squad
Durcan blurted out: "Poet."

In fact, Durcan could just as credibly
Have retorted "Salesman"
For all the trim aplomb
Of the clobber he was sporting:
Herringbone tweed jacket,
Blue button-down shirt,
Black slacks, black shoes.
The security chap stared hard at Durcan:
"I didn't catch that, sir."
Durcan reiterated: "Poet."

The security chap
Between stapled lips
Levelled his tongue:
"What is your business in the United Kingdom, sir?"
"I was reading poetry yesterday afternoon in Cheltenham."
The security chap put his hand inside his own jacket:
"I asked you your business in the United Kingdom, sir?"
"I was reading poetry yesterday afternoon in Cheltenham."
"Are you an author?"
"Yes, I am an author."
"You publish books under your own name?"
'Yes, I do publish books under my own name."
"Can you tell me the name of one of these books of yours?"
Durcan elephantinely replies: "*A Snail in My Prime*."

I could see the wrist of the security chap's hand
Tighten under his jacket.
Durcan primly unzipped his black leather reverend mother's
     handbag
And produced a large paperback volume entitled
A Snail in My Prime.
He closed his eyes and launched himself into a poem.
He began to sway, shake, loll his head:
"I'm always here, if you want me;
I am the centre of the universe."

Like a scrum-half trying to shovel out impossible ball
The officer gesticulated helplessly with his two hands
For Durcan to pass on
But Durcan was neither seeing nor hearing anybody.
The officer was getting frantic to let Durcan through
But he could not. Another passenger behind me –
A young man with long black hair in a ponytail –
Shouted out to a small red-haired beauty beside him:
"That's Paul Durcan, Mother, that's Paul Durcan"
But the mother hissed "Shsh, Jason, shsh."
Two police officers in flak jackets with sub-machine guns
And Alsatian dogs on chained leashes stood behind the small
     crowd,
The security officer signalling to them not to intervene.
When Durcan finished we all broke into a nervous applause
Including the security officer
Who, as promptly as he decently could, said:
"Thank you, sir. I hope you have a pleasant journey."

As he strode on, head goose-high in the air,
Durcan stumbled
And I – as I passed the security officer –
I could *hear* the froth on the hairs of his testicles.
I could *see* the froth on the hairs of his testicles.

Here was one Irish subversive that British Security
Would probably, certainly, happily liquidate –
You look like a walking urine sample
I remonstrated with Durcan as we fastened our safety belts.
Durcan smiled that silly-filly smile of his
Informing me that if our Fokker 50 crashed
On a rocky island in the Irish Sea
He'd be happy to drink his own urine.
Phenomenal thirst these poet chaps have.

Paddy Dwyer

Vona, how I envy Paddy Dwyer!

Paddy Dwyer has his own
Shoe shop in Drogheda –
Paddy Dwyer's of Shop Street.
If I'd known what I was about
When I set out to be a poet
Up the road from Edgeworthstown
I'd have walked for ten years
In the footsteps of Paddy Dwyer.
I'd have served my time
Not in the literary pubs of Dublin
And London but in a shoe shop
In Dusseldorf or Nimes
And in the course of time
Set up shop in a country town
With upstairs my books and my
CD Radio Cassette Recorder.

I'd have wanted to be
A great lyric, rhyming poet
Up there with Yeats and Keats,
With Pushkin and Baudelaire.
Therefore I'd have emulated Paddy Dwyer
And sold quality shoes at affordable prices:
Bally, Nike and K.
I'd have worked out front in my shop
With my sleeves rolled up selling shoes;
Welcoming customers, making customers
Feel unique, equal, wanted.

Like you, Vona, and your husband Conor
I'd have wanted you to feel
Like myself about feet –
That feet have hill-top cities
In their Italies called toes;
That feet are of the first water;
That feet are different;
That feet are serious;
That no two pairs of feet are the same;
That feet are vulnerable;
That feet can get gangrene;
That feet have minds of their own;
That knees are peacocks
That stoop in their tails;
That shoes are tiaras;
That I am king of my shop;
That every customer is an Infant Christ
Before whom I must kneel down and adore;
Caress his feet on a footstool;
Tie up his laces.

I'd have courted a country girl
From the heart of Meath –
From Yellow Furze –
With a heart of gold like Roslyn
Who works in the Peter Mark hairdressing salon
In Drogheda Town Centre.
I'd have concentrated on affection and business –
The business of affection –
And on the horticulture of shoes.

I'd have let the poetry look after itself
In my home above the shop;
Late at night in the a.m.

In the cage of my patience;
My portable typewriter on the kitchen table,
My wife asleep in the next room;
The spine of Michael Hartnett
Looking sideways at me
From the top shelf of the dresser;
The ghost of Nano Reid
Luminous over the kitchen sink;
I'd have cultivated
Only those brands of poems
That demand cultivation.

Having got to know other men's feet
After my own
Maybe I'd have had the compassion
To write for my townsman
The song of his soul
And still like Paddy Dwyer
Opened a second shop across the street
Selling ladies' shoes.
Stiller and stiller.
I'd have had to get to know ladies' feet;
Without presumption or arrogance known
Myself the equal of Owen and Shearer,
Ronaldo and Dunga.

Instead at fifty-two here I am
Not only without a home
But without a shoe shop of my own;
With only a shoestring to my name.
What hope have I of writing a poem
Without a shoe shop of my own?
Not to mention a home?

I look into the busy, chuffed face of Paddy Dwyer,
Affable, ruddy, watery, crackling,
Those hectic, steely eyes
Dreaming dreams, seeing visions
Of Leeds United
As he shoehorns my feet
Into a pair of Ks –
Black leather slip-ons –
And ask myself am I likely
Ever to write poems
As well-made, yet casual?
As light, yet durable?
Shall I ever be quite the poet on fire
As is the shoe-shop man Paddy Dwyer?

Vona, how I envy Paddy Dwyer!

Tinkerly Luxemburgo

to Bill Swainson

My name is Tinkerly Luxemburgo –
I am a slave to my work.
Oh, take the day off, hop into the car,
Drive out to the Shopping Centre,
Park in the Shopping Centre Carpark,
Go for a saunter in Roches Stores.
It is as good as going swimming –
Going for a saunter in Roche's Stores;
The up escalator, the down escalator;
Floating the levels.

If you are going to be lonely,
Be lonely in style.

I snap up a pair of white cords
And – to match –
A white shirt, white briefs,
White shoes, white socks;
Drive back home in the slow lane,
Relish cars overtaking me,
Tune in to the Gay Byrne Show –
Middle-aged men insisting
That they are above sex, protesting
That they are beyond sex.
Funny. I laugh
Lashings when I'm lonely.

If you are going to be lonely,
Be lonely in style.

I change into my purchases,
Grab the duster and Brasso,
Open the hall door and stand
On the footpath with my back
To the street and begin
Dusting my knocker.
For a whole hour I dust
My brass knocker, every grain
And gleam of it, every stain
And shadow of it,
Dust it around and around, down
And up, up and down.

If you're going to be lonely,
Be lonely in style.

I spit on my knocker
And without turning round once
I can feel every passing motorist
Taking note of me as I lean
Into my door and sway under
My door and bury my head
In my door and gaze up
At my door and kneel down
At my door and pray at my door –
My very own wailing wall.
God, I would love to be proposed to
By Oscar Wilde.

If you are going to be lonely,
Be lonely in style.

I spotted a largish man today in Roches Stores
Enquiring for a pair of goggles.
Swimming goggles – he sang in a restrained bass.
He purchased a swimcap also.
And a box of earplugs. And one noseclip.
The spitting image of Oscar Wilde.
I could see him composing
All alone in a flat in Merrion Square
The Soul of Man under Socialism
And standing on the high diving board
And gripping his heretical book under his cheeky bottom
And diving backwards down into Westland Row
And going missing like a papal banker
For a purgatory of ten or eleven seconds
Only to surface like a baby whale
All spouting, swallowing, spitting,
And singing out my name – Tinkerly!
Tinkerly Luxemburgo!

If you are going to be lonely,
Be lonely in style.

Tangier in Winter

Nothing in the villa works except the faucets
And the ballcock which I've propped up with bottles.
All is silent all day every day all winter
Except for the sobbing of Bacon's laughter:
First thing in the morning, last thing at night,
The grand laughter,
The J. M.W. Turner steam train of exclamation marks
!!!!!!!!!!!!!!!!!!!!!!
As Bacon sits on his stool, bent over,
His left leg thrown across his right knee,
Squealing, choking, howling,
Repeating over and over:
Endsville !!!!!!!!!!!!!!!!!!!!!
Endsville !!!!!!!!!!!!!!!!!!!!!

II

I sunbathe outside on the patio overlooking the beach
In the first and last of the sun
Reading the Penguin paperback edition of *The Fall* by Camus
With my back to the French doors of the salon
Where in one corner a cairn of champagne bottles
Has been by Bacon most tidily piled.

Out in the desert camels go round and round
Lunging in the camel pound.

In the doorway
Bacon appears in the pink –

In the pink buff
With a kisscurl in his quiff.
He carries out a carafe of iced water
Pours two drops of it onto my two knees.
Gingerly he places the spout to my lips:
He murmurs: "I will school you
To drink the lees –
To sip the lees ever so
Keenly and slowly –
Keenly and slowly."

Out in the desert the camels go round and round
Lunging in the camel pound.

Cissy Young's

to Rosa Alice Branco

That first year in Cork city – '71/'72 –
I spent the afternoons from four to six
Sitting alone sipping pints of Smithwicks
In a public house on the Bandon Road,
Cissy Young's,
Reading Bishop Berkeley's *A Treatise
Concerning the Principles of Human Knowledge.*
I, ex-footballer, ex-hurler, ex-high-jumper,
Branded by the dominant males
Of the Irish tribe "a hippy",
Rejoiced in the eighteenth-century,
Metaphysical atmosphere of Cissy Young's.
I sat in the private lounge,
As distinct from the public bar,
Because the private lounge was nearly always empty.
Men in the public bar saluted me
Through the hatch.
Cissy Young's, all formica, banquette,
More anonymous, cosier by far
Than any salty, arty Kinsale bar.

That year in Cissy Young's reading Berkeley
Was a foundation year in my life as a writer
And, if I may meekly, profoundly trumpet,
My life as the virtuoso university teacher
I never became:
An attacking player on Berkeley's dream team.
Cissy Young's on the Bandon Road

Was my University of the Bermudas
Where I learnt the basics of my trade:
Learnt to think the hard way;
Learnt how to head the ball one way, looking the other
    way;
Learnt the relationship between soul and body;
Learnt to communicate through the hatch;
Learnt how to introduce Libyan storytellers to Cork
    insurance officials;
Learnt that reality is poetry, poetry reality;
Learnt the way of all things;
Learnt the existence of God –
That at five in the afternoon
On the Bandon Road in Cork City in Ireland
In the empty, private lounge of Cissy Young's
"To be is to be perceived."

Notes Towards a Supreme Reality

I

Because the supreme reality in life is fiction
It is vital not to meet the writer in person.
There is no necessary linkage between the egotist who is
        overweight and vain
And the magic connections, dreams, constructions of his brain.

II

Life's supreme reality is reading fiction
In poetry or prose, most likely prose,
(Fiction is scarce as water in poetry);
Afterwards telephoning Niall MacMonagle in Rathmines,
Conversing nonstop for three hours,
Putting on aerial displays for our sleeping daughters,
Flying low, fast, looping the loop;
Or taking a Super Low Floor
Green Engine Kneeling Suspension
Dublin Bus into the city centre
To Cormac Kinsella in the Dublin Waterstone's,
Stealing an half-hour with Cormac behind the bookshelves.

Thanks to Cormac Kinsella
I have spent the last five years
Reading Richard Ford and Don DeLillo.
Oh yes! Behind the bookshelves!
Like two haymakers siesta-ing
Behind a haycock in Provence
Cormac and I –
We repose vertically in a Ford sun

Cooled by a De Lillo breeze
Analysing the universals of light,
The particulars of power.

III

The evening is as long as life is short.
Reading *Independence Day* or *Underworld*
I am a tern detecting Dublin Bay
At a cruising altitude of thirteen feet;
Or a flock of swallows on a warm June evening
Trawling to and fro the mown lawn
Netting succulent midges, snaring thousands of 'em.
The evening is as long as life is short.

Tea-Drinking with the Gods

The telephone rings and I squeeze open my eyes.
My publisher tells me that he has sold the rights
To all the poetry I have ever written
For one hundred and seventy three pounds
And fifty pence. My beloved beside me in bed
With her back turned to me tells me
She plans to spend Christmas with her son.
Driving out the gate I catch my tail light
On the gate post and hear a short, sharp crunch.
In the newsagents when I stammer Good Morning
The newsagent does not hear me.
In the post office the postmistress
Insists that there is no mail for me.
My mother when I visit her for lunch
Scolds me that I do not eat enough.
When I decline her Ambrosia rice pudding
She casts up her eyes to heaven.

At 7 p.m. I arrive at the National Gallery
To give a poetry reading.
I stand up in front of five hundred people
And recite for an hour and fifteen minutes
Wondering if I will ever get to the end.
My mind is on other things.
In today's newspaper the British Government states
That its private stance is the same as its public stance.
Halfway through the reading a man in the audience
Stands up, walks up to the microphone
And whispers into my ear: Where is the toilet?
He walks out of the hall and two poems later

Walks back in with two bottles of whiskey.
At the end of the reading there are waves of applause.
People milling around me with books
To be autographed. One middle-aged couple
Trying to come forward, reluctant, reticent,
The husband pressing a carrier bag into my hand
Explaining: "My wife made this for you."

I walk home alone in dark, wet, cold,
Past the palings of Merrion Square,
Past hundreds of silent spear-carriers;
Down the canyon of Mount Street,
Down along the Grand Canal,
Past Kitty O'Shea's,
Past the empty gasholders
Down along South Lotts Road,
Through the deserted streets of Ringsend and Irishtown.
When I get in the door and switch on the light
The light does not come on. Another bulb gone
And I forgot to get spare bulbs
And I bet the battery in the torch is dead.

But the battery is not dead. The battery is alive.
By the light of the torch
I investigate the contents of the carrierbag,
A creased Post Office carrierbag.
Out of wads of tissue
Struggles a tea-cosy,
A patchwork tea-cosy
With in red thread
Three words stitched:
CRAZY ABOUT PAUL.
I stand alone in the dark
Staring up at the street lamp
Through the dust-iced fanlight

Before tramping up to bed.
Between the sheets,
My spout sticking out.
Cosy, cosily, cosiness.
Wholly alive, wholly dead.

Buswells Hotel, Molesworth Street

Colleen, will you do me a favour?
One last favour before I die?
Before there is peace in Ireland?
One last favour in 1993?
In the worst year of my life?
In the year when my hands began
To tremble for no reason?
When my tongue fell down into my tummy?
And my memory started to hang back
As if it were shy of the past
And massacres became two a penny
And my business partner who was my friend
Sold up our business behind my back
And my true love grew weary of me?
Will you do me one last favour?
One last favour which if you would
You would bring such a smile to my face,
Such mint, such sage of mirth,
That I would surge through parliament gates
With my head held high
And if the police asked me the number of my car
And I could not remember it I would not get flustered
But I would stumble in my own time
Slowly to the rear of my car, bend down,
Fumbling with my bifocals, stammer
To read the reg. no. off the rear number plate
Em Em 92 MH 2185?
You will? One last favour?
Meet me in Buswells Hotel in Molesworth Street!

For what? I don't know for what.
Only a hotel to go to in Molesworth Street
And for an hour to be a couple of Buswells.

Self-Portrait '95

Paul Durcan would try the patience of the Queen of Tonga.
When he was in Copacabana he was homesick for
   Annaghmakerrig;
When he got back to Annaghmakerrig
He was homesick for Copacabana.

Ashplant, New Year's Eve, 1996

Year in, year out, I tramp Sandymount Strand.
Is there no one to talk to in Ireland?

We Believe in Hurling

to Mícheál Ó Súilleabháin

I have such a craving for thee, O Donal Óg,
Because you praise my days with hurling deeds;
When you make leaps with your back to the goals
Plucking high balls out of teeming skies
To hurl them low between the posts;
Deeds alone are certain good.

3.15 p.m. Sunday afternoon
In the bar of the Slievemore Hotel
On the side of the flapping mountain
Pegged down in cloud.
Red-eyed with grief, perched
On a high stool at the bar,
I am staring up into a blank screen.

Will nobody switch it on –
The TV up there on its black bracket?
Have I come out in vain
In the gale and the rain?
Do none of you here believe
In the All Ireland Hurling Final
Between Tipperary and Clare?

If I ask – if I ask
The man behind the bar
To switch on the television
Will he? My scepticism
Whispers: Maybe he will not.

He smiles a barman's Japanese smile.
Pictures alight on the screen

Like birds on the bough.
The woods of Croke Park are alive!
The hurlers of Tipperary and Clare
Are warming up in the goals.
Like young fillies at Ascot
At the starting gate prancing;
All halters, all helmets.

For seventy deluged minutes
I do not budge from my stool.
I roost on my stool
Making faces at the screen;
Big faces, little faces
At each orbit-of-the-earth trajectory of the ball;
Catch, cut, puck, double, solo, hop.

These are the boys who were born
To sweeten and delight;
To bejewel and beautify.
I laugh, I gasp, I frown.
At the final whistle
I jump down to my feet,
Hug myself.

I stride over to the TV.
I stand under its black bracket
Gazing up at the Great Loughnane
Being interrogated about the game.
Tears alight in my eyes
As I listen to him rhapsodize
That it was the game that won the game.

He cries: "The game of hurling
Is pure poetry.
Pure inspiration. Pure technique.
Hurling won the game today,
Not Tipperary, not Clare.
Today we saw the greatest game
Of hurling we will ever see."

I stride out of the bar
Into the gale and the rain
And I hasten off up into the mountain
Bareheaded, open-necked
Into the fuchsia, into the montbretia;
Into the stick-boss solitudes:
As free as a man can ever be.

Hurling is the father of freedom.
When Jamesie O'Connor with a minute to go
At full tilt in the middle of the park
Pointed for Clare
Spacemen on *Mir* saw Planet Earth
Fly up out of its tree.
The hurler strikes, and man is free.

I have such a craving for thee, O Donal Óg,
Because you praise my days with hurling deeds;
When you make leaps with your back to the goals
Plucking high balls out of teeming skies
To hurl them low between the posts;
Deeds alone are certain good.

14 SEPTEMBER 1997

123

Surely My God Is Kavanagh

to John McHugh

A horse and cab drives up to the Grand Canal
At Baggot Street Bridge. Out scramble
Five foxes – five scented young ladies –
Over from Liverpool for a weekend in Dublin
Barking to pose for photographs on the seat
Alongside the bronze poet Kavanagh.

The first blonde sits beside Kavanagh
With her hand on his knee, well above his knee;
The second blonde stands behind Kavanagh
With her hand on his head,
Her false nails plucking his eyebrows;
The third blonde sits the other side of Kavanagh
With her cheek against his cheek,
Giving him a long, full kiss on the lips;
The two redheads stand sentinel smirking
Either side of the tableau.

The second blonde murmurs to Kavanagh:
"What do you like, honey?"
Kavanagh reflects: "Women with fivers."
Second blonde: "This is my fourth time in Ibiza."
Kavanagh: "Are there any locals in Ibiza?"
"All the time – Ibiza is full of Scousers."

The five ladies ride off into the sun at noon
Low in the sky of a November day,
Heading for the Rowley Mile –

Leeson Street, Merrion Row.
Along the towpath stroll
A couple in their thirties
With baby in pram and a six-year-old
Fair-haired, blue-eyed, curly-headed boy
Whom they hail as Sebastian
Shrieking at the height of his bent:
"May I sit on his knee?
May I sit on his foot?
May I climb up his leg?
May I stand on his tummy?"

The little boy plays with the bronze poet
Until mum and dad – more mum than dad –
Coax him away and a courting couple
Stroll up and she unsheathes a camera – an Olympus –
And asks her man to sit beside the poet
But her man is shy and he tiptoes behind the seat
To cringe bashfully behind the poet.
She remonstrates with him and he yields
And crawls back around and slides down
Into the seat with embarrassment
Scratching the back of his neck,
Glancing up at the poet beside him
To ask for permission:
"Nobody sitting here, is there?"

The bronze poet seated with arms folded
Shakes his head and smiles
That infinitely baffled, infinitely affectionate,
Other-galaxy smile of his
And resumes talking to himself:
"I am fulfilled because the canal is fulfilled."

Across the canal on the opposite bank
Over the heads of three swans and half-a-hundred ducks
On a seat erected by Dublin Tourism
Old locals delight to watch the goings-on,
Observe that the bronze poet is an honoured soul,
Catch his soliloquy on the soul-caressing breeze:
"A tourist attraction! Well, you don't tell me!"

Surely my God is Kavanagh!
Who is content with feeding praise to the good.
While other poets my comic light resent
The spirit that is Kavanagh caresses my soul.

23 NOVEMBER 1997

On First Hearing News of
Patrick Kavanagh

October 1960, Gonzaga College, Dublin:
"Boys" – Father Joseph Veale, SJ, joins
Together in a steeple his long, cloistral fingers –
Our teacher whom we'd trust with our lives –
Our tall, dark, enigmatic man in whom
Are spliced in a thrilling, glamorous mix
Gravity and levity –
"Boys – thank you, Paul, yes, open the window –
You all know my distrust of the word 'phoney';
Well, I don't like saying it but poetry
Or, I should say, what passes
For modern poetry is phoney
Or strikes me as phoney. In our country only
Patrick Kavanagh strikes me as genuine
And in America William Carlos Williams
Whose 'Flowers by the Sea' you will remember
I chalked up on the blackboard in April.
Yeats for all his indubitable mastery of rhetoric
Strikes me as nailed down to a trick.
Alas, you will hear, if you have not already heard,
People make unkind, cruel even,
Cuts about Patrick Kavanagh;
I have heard an urbane, honourable senator state:
'Patrick Kavanagh is an absolute lunatic.'
When I protested the senator added:
'Patrick Kavanagh would talk to anything.'

"Myself, I have seen with my own eyes
Patrick Kavanagh conversing with trees

On Waterloo Road.
As I walked past, I thought to myself:
There is a man in touch with reality.
Poetry, I believe, when it is not phoney,
Is – like Milton – the figure of reality.
What I thought the trees were saying to Patrick Kavanagh
     was:
'Come Dance With Kitty Stobling'
Which, as it happens, is the name
Of Patrick Kavanagh's most recent volume
Published by Longmans in London.
But boys – please take note –
It was not a one-way conversation.
Patrick Kavanagh was talking to the trees –
Yes, he was – in down-to-earth, matter-of-fact, everyday
     tones;
But the trees also were talking to Patrick Kavanagh
In similar vein – in down-to-earth, matter-of-fact, everyday
     tones.
Now, let us resume *Paradise Lost*."

Waterloo Road

On Waterloo Road on an August day
I met Patrick Kavanagh in his garden flat.
After I rang the bell there was a long pause –
To open . . . or not to open –
Before I identified two sad, wise, humourous eyes
In black horn
Peering out at me through the spyhole window high up in
       the door.

Patrick Kavanagh led me up the long hall
To the living room at the back looking out on the garden.
He sat down in an ocean-going armchair of a past era
With dozens of anthologies of American poetry
In stacks round about his shoeless feet on the floor.
He blinked up into the skies behind me:
"The American anthology is great for the kickstart."
We sat in silence – two deferential elephants.
He the old cobbler at the term of his days;
I the young apprentice in my first pregnancy.
"The apprenticeship," he declared eagerly, sitting out forward
"The apprenticeship, you know, is twenty years."

It was a golden day on Waterloo Road –
Blue skies, shirt sleeves, bicycles, miniskirts –
As we strolled down to the Waterloo House
Past Michael Kane's big window for a lunchtime drink.
There was an anticyclone over Ireland.
At the construction site on the corner of Waterloo Road
That was to become the office block of the Yellow Pages
Patrick Kavanagh halted with his hands on his hips

Gazing up at the meteoric men in yellow hats
Walking tightropes smoking fags.
From them to me he switched gaze solemnly.
Divining the mystery of the universe, he announced:
"Men at Work!" He tossed his head back. "Men at Work!"

That day Patrick Kavanagh had a wedding to go to
In the Shangri-La Hotel on the hill of Dalkey.
Through the armies of the sun we rode a taxi
Like Lenny Bruce and Billy the Kid
In a chariot along the shore of Dublin Bay.
Although I was homeless, jobless, futureless,
I felt wholly safe in Patrick Kavanagh's company.
I uttered: "Today is such a golden day
It reminds me of days I stayed in the monastery –
The Trappist Monastery at Mount Melleray."

Consternation in the back of the taxi.
Patrick Kavanagh groaned:
"On a summer's day like today
Don't be thinking about monasteries.
On a summer's day like today
You should be thinking about beautiful women."
When in the lobby of the Shangri-La
The head waiter spotted us
He took us for a pair of winos,
Made to throw us out,
Only for the bridegroom to rescue us.
Patrick Kavanagh was the guest of honour.

Humming snatches of "On Raglan Road"
Patrick Kavanagh sat down on a couch behind me –
"For that I'll vouch on any couch" –
While I, sitting up at the bar, found

Myself beside a beautiful woman
With long red hair, green eyes, freckles.
Nessa O'Neill was her name and she invited me
To go for a swim with her at the bottom of the garden.
The Shangri-La backed on to the Irish Sea.
There was an Indian Summer that year in Ireland
And in October she and I set up home in London.
We lived together sixteen years,
 Rearing two golden girls.

On Waterloo Road on the first of August I met her first and knew
That her red hair would weave a snare that I would never rue;
I embraced the danger, I sailed along in the enchanted cab
And I rowed my oar by the star of Patrick Kavanagh.

Patrick Kavanagh at *Tarry Flynn*,
the Abbey Theatre, 1967

Where the devil did I put me cap?
Every night at eight o'clock on the dot
I take a taxi from the Bailey public house
Soberly sozzled, never noxiously stocious,
North across the Liffey to the Abbey Theatre
Where my *Tarry Flynn* has been playing for over a year –
Playing to full houses. In the back seat of the taxi
I join hands on my belly, incline my head to my left,
Incline my head to my right, gazing out the windows,
Giving the passers-by my salute and my blessing.
In my time I have known presidents and archbishops
But did any of them know this kind of suzerainty?
I am a suzerain honoured in my sulky streets
Playing to full houses for over a year.
Ye can't say it often enough, can ye?
Playing to full houses for over a year!

As I gaze out the taxi windows at the middling-to-good faces
Of the ordinary, decent heroes and heroines of my parish
Hurrying home in the rain under lamplight
Clutching string-tied barm bracks in force-nine gales
I observe them bowing to me and they are beseeching me:
Paddy Paddy Paddy Paddy Paddy
Come on in home into the Fifth Estate of Suburbia.

While the box office count my share of the day's takings –
The author's sacred ten per cent –
I sit in the back stalls watching young Donal McCann
Playing me as I was when I was twenty-three –

The same age then as he is now
And I, like an ould, black, shaggy tomcat
In my sack of sixty-two years, am lifted up dripping
Into the gods of ecstasy – not the frenzy of power,
Not the hysteria of possession,
But the freedom of the audience.
We are all members of the audience,
If we only knew it.

Young McCann grew up in the suburbs of Dublin,
Yet he catches me better
Than I could catch myself;
He has gutted me of that sickly sentiment
That has been the bane of my bastardly days;
Gutted me of begobbery; boggery; bardery.
Instead he has caught the universal thing –
The purgatorial boy under his mother's wing.

Thanks to young McCann
For the first time in my life
I have a daily income
And am in debt to no man!
Oh how skippily he treads those boards!
Skippily as I did trod those fields!
Sticking his big toe
Into a little mystery!

In a minute I will collect my ten per cent cut.
At the end of my life kyboshed in the back stalls
My baby soul is bobbing in death's waves rearing to go!
Where the devil did I put me cap?

"Snatch Out of Time
the Passionate Transitory"

I

After the golden summer of '67 –
Patrick Kavanagh's *annus mirabilis* –
Wellbeing, rude health, good humour, good friends –
Matrimony, race meetings, the garden flat –
Prospects better than they'd ever been –
The death of Patrick Kavanagh
Was a box in the bollox –
To coin a phrase
He himself coined to the taxi driver
Outside the Shangri-La Hotel.
Patrick Kavanagh was a lyric poet.

On the night of November the thirtieth
Patrick Kavanagh's friend Brian Lynch
Remarked to me he'd heard rumours
That Patrick Kavanagh had taken ill.
As we sat over pints of Phoenix
In Dwyer's of Lower Leeson Street
Pondering the significance of rumours
Patrick Kavanagh lay dying
Round the corner in Herbert Street
On the second floor of a nursing home.

Early next morning my bedroom door
Was rattled open by my mother who marched
To the end of my bed and who said:
Patrick Kavanagh is dead.

I traipsed past the corpse laid out in the nursing home,
That noble, sophisticated skull in repose.
Oh how Patrick Kavanagh adored that word:
Repose repose repose repose repose.

II

There was only one way – one way I could face
The death of Patrick Kavanagh
And that was to become Patrick Kavanagh myself.
At the front of the top deck
Of the number 13 bus
My mother passed me in the afternoon
Standing on the corner of Lower Leeson Street
Outside Joe Dwyer's public house
My hands on my hips,
My head tossed back,
Pronouncing, sighing, beseeching, provoking,
Divining the mysteries of the universe
For the passers-by.
After a year's grieving I became myself –
The poet Patrick Kavanagh had invited me to be:
A soul in repose, come what may.

The Who's Who of Irish Poetry

Who *is* Patrick Kavanagh?
The Elizabeth Bishop of Inniskeen.
A fifty-year-long prize fight with addiction;
Two dozen poems nearing completion.

Kavanagh's Ass

She borrowed the loan of Kavanagh's ass
To bring her grandson to first Mass:
Despite the stutter in my tongue
I was the Estonia of her eye.

Between the hill farm and the chapel
Reeled two miles of Mayo streets;
Hedgerows skinnier than Tallinn skyscrapers;
Bogs dozing in Baltic fog.

She shouldered me up onto the back of the ass,
Slotting my feet into stirrups;
She walked me all the way to chapel
With the halter like bracelets round her wrist.

We tethered the ass to the chapel railing,
Stood back in the frost and gave him
One long, last, beseeching glance
Before burrowing off into Mass.

In Kavanagh's ass I saw the nose of my soul
Peering back out at me
In drenched Estonian exile
And I knew as I entered

Into fifty years of folly
That neither Herod nor Pilate –
Be his name Durcan or Eichman –
Could ever bully me

Because, like Kavanagh's ass,
I am the gap in the ditch;
I am an alp of speechlessness;
I am your inamorata pining for your sealed oath.

Francis Bacon's Double Portrait
of Patrick Kavanagh

Slide One

Hobo on banquette in Bloomsbury pub,
Peasant's shoulders bent to Museum Street;
"The enormous tragedy of whose dream";
Low winter sunlight shooting in
Saloon bar window from behind;
Mongrel dogs of compassion and pity
Lolling on waters of smile;
Inner man visible to crudest eye;
Outer man universally invisible
But for gorilla silhouette
Juggling pairs of horn-rimmed spectacles;
Queen bee of megasoul
Observing worker bees of word-pan
Accumulating nectar and pollen.

Slide Two

The infant caged in the bestiality
          of an old man's body
Crying out for help – crying out
          to be rescued
As the tide of death climbs higher
          and higher
Around the rock of his fate.

The King of Cats

to Francis Stuart on his 95th Birthday

Francis – on a Friday evening in Dundrum
At the curtain of the twentieth century –
Dares me to be a child again:
"Imagine being Dostoyevsky..."
(*Pause*) "Or a gnat." Lucky me
To be sitting in the company of a dead man.

How many years ago is it since you died?
You have always been a cat but since your death
A before-only-sniffed-at flexibility buzzes your fuzz
Entitling you to enlighten me in the evolution of flight –
To give me a gnat's-eye glimpse of the cosmos
And of Russian fiction – the last word in death.

Over twenty golden years
We have spent hundreds of hours in silence
Confronting one another in your shadowy living room
Over coffee and cheese
From five to seven
On the lookout for words.

I visit you at rush hour.
Rush hour! – you exclaim
Pawing the phrase
Before dousing it in laughter:
That skimming, cormorant chuckle
Halfway between a revelation and a peep.

Goodbye, Francis – see you soon.
See you soon, Paul – you cry out.

In my car at your gate I perch in the dark
Under the orange streetlight a gnat in an Astra
Facing downhill to The Great Wall Of China –
Your local corner takeaway – and the Scots pines
High above the Central Mental Hospital kremlin walls.
I can hear a spade undressing clay

Or is it the blackbird in your snowdrops –
The blackbird you announced to me when I came –
"The first blackbird of Spring"?
I switch on the ignition – glance
Back over at the switched-on porch light of your home.
Yet again I have visited your tomb and found it empty.

The Stoning of Francis Stuart

It was a dark, cold day,
Empty, windy, wet,
The day of the stoning
Of Francis Stuart.

January the sixth,
Nineteen ninety-eight,
Eleven a.m.
Stoning Old River Man.

It was a St Patrick's Day
Parade kind of day;
The police erected
Crowd control barriers.

Thanks to friends
Of enemies, we had seats
At a fifth-floor window
Of a Temple Bar weekly.

Down below us
Fleet Street
Was empty and silent
But for the Stoning Catwalk.

Motorcycle cops
Accelerating, stopping;
Blue sirens of police cars
Whirling, swirling.

When Francis Stuart
Was led out
He looked more than
His ninety-five years.

He had been on the run
In the Wicklow mountains;
Blackthorn to blackthorn;
Nursing home to nursing home.

But although he was carried,
Or half-carried out,
When he came to his spot
He stood upright, unaided.

In a pair of new, yellow underpants
He cut a spinsterish figure:
Potbelly billowing out
Over spindly legs;

Wispy white hair
Strewn like aftermath
Over bone-structure in which
Bobbed a shrivelled, black penis;

Jolly journalist next me
Whispered in Anglo-Irishese:
"Would fetch a pretty penny
At auction – Stuart's dicky."

Round the Stoning Plinth
The chief critics of Ireland
Stood in a line,
Each with an arty stone.

As for the stoning itself
It was oddly boring;
It was hard to maintain
One's concentration.

It was like being
At a matinée,
Or at a bullfight –
Deadly but dull.

One's eyes straying.
There was a microphone
Stapled to Stuart's ear
But he screamed nothing.

Some thought they could hear
The old man humming
The Edith Piaf song:
Je ne regrette rien.

He staggered and fell,
Half stood up and crawled;
Waved his hands in the air,
Vomited and shat.

I found myself staring
At the faces of the critics
As each of them took
Their turn to stone him.

The chief critics,
As chief critics will,
Put little effort
Into their stoning.

The chief critics
Were half-hearted,
Quarter-hearted,
In their stoning;

Devoid of dexterity.
The chief critics
Missed the target,
Blushed guiltily.

The chief-chief critics
Wore homespun balaclavas;
With clenched mittens
Warming their groins with their stones.

The chief-chief critics
Aimed for the head;
Principally pranging
The frontal lobes.

Finally, it came
To the turn of the paramount
Chief-chief critic of Ireland:
A tall, dark, young man

With a wedge moustache
On the upper lip
Of his elf-beak,
Like a fast bowler

With a Cork arm,
A Cork accent,
A Cork wrist-action,
A Cork frenzy,

He took a long
Run up before
Letting fly a rasper,
Scoring a bull's eye:

Knocking out Stuart's middle stump;
A yorker between the eyes;
Boring a small pink hole
In the nonagenarian reprobate's forehead.

The buttons of his underpants flew off
Exposing ancient buttocks
Which from behind looked
Like a girl model's face:

A pair of cheeks
In a looking glass;
Mandolin-shaped;
Pale, smooth;

Carol's bottom
In profile
Styled, cleaved
By Brian of London.

He toppled off the plinth.
It was fun
Watching him
Cartwheeling backwards.

After he'd been quite stoned to death
There was the ritual kicking.
The critics of Ireland queued up
To give Stuart a kick each.

Tedious too but curious.
One middle-aged leatherclad female skinhead
Made a bags of kicking in Stuart's head.
Instead she kicked out his Adam's apple.

Meek, strident cries of
"Old bollox" and
"Old fart"
Squeaked in the wind.

Bits of Stuart in puddles…
Polite applause
Trickled out of the crowd
Up along Fleet Street

Into the front office
Of the Temple Bar weekly,
Up the stairs and into
The editor's office.

An assistant editor –
In the middle of an editorial
Conference on men's fashions –
Franked his pad with a spit;

Picked his nose,
Stared at his fellow editors
Watching him nose-picking,
Ticked his spit with his red biro.

I am considering it;
I am not a nitwit;
A minute – while I deposit
My mucus under my armpit.

My Marks & Sparks mucus;
Microwave mucus.
Our line is clean on it;
Stuart is a shit.

After Stuart's corpse
Was humped away
To be dumped
In an unmarked grave

Under a chip-shop wall
Between the Central
Mental Hospital
And the Luas light railway line

The chief critics
Of a totally united Ireland
Held hands in a daisy-chain
Under Oscar Wilde's statue

While a bonfire was made
Of Stuart's books;
Although none of them
Had ever read Stuart's books

It was felt that etiquette demanded
Suart's books be burned;
At the sight of *A Hole in the Head*
And *Memorial,*

The High Consistory,
Redemption, Pillar of Cloud,
Things to Remember,
We Have Kept the Faith

And, of course, most of all
Black List, Section H
All going up in flames
The critics' souls were warmed.

As Stuart's last book burned
The chat was not of Stuart
But of next week's dinner
To honour Salman Rushdie.

'Twas a noble idee
To beg The Beestie
To do a head of Rushdie:
'Twas a noble idee!

'Tis a gladsome orgy
Of bad faith I'll organize;
Stuart's great granddaughter
With smackeroons I'll flatterize.

Taxis were finger-snapped
For Malahide and Churchtown;
The consciences of the playboys
Of the nation rode home

To their sub-suburban estates;
Before fornication hour
To watch themselves on the nine o'clock news
Stoning to death Francis Stuart.

"Good evening, here is the News:
In Dublin this afternoon
Despite heavy rain and gale-force winds
The ninety-five-year-old writer,

Francis Stuart, was stoned to death
By his critics.
Reports afterward indicated
That it was an average stoning.

In Mullingar prices
For cattle and pigs dropped
By point three of a Euro;
The Euro Bank is not to issue a statement."

Making myself comfy
Between sheets and pillows
I svent to svleep sviling:
Stones skimming into Stuart's puss

Is such a satisfying image.
We forgot to drown Stuart's cat –
Black Minnaloushe.
That was remiss of us.

"Alone, important and wise"
Yeats used call Stuart's cat
That sat always in Stuart's lap;
"Alone, important and wise".

Dancing with Brian Friel

to Brian Friel on his 70th birthday

Quarter-way down the wrought-iron staircase
Of Waterstone's bookshop in Dublin
I see down below me on the far left
At the Irish Drama counter
Brian Friel browsing.
I must not say hallo.
Man at Browse: Do Not Disturb.

I have not seen him for twenty years.
Real Inishowen man!
At seventy, how quick he looks!
In a danced-in, linen, creamy, summer suit,
Blue shirt open at the neck, white T-shirt,
On-shore-leave sailor dancing the bookshops!
Tracking the steps of Gene Kelly, Fred Astaire,
Shuffling sideways the shelves,
Tapping exits, entrances.

My little bull of Affection begins to bellow
And without ado
Crashes through my thicket of Etiquette.
In the *Galateo* of '99
Monsignore Paolo della Casa falls at the first!

We exchange smoke signals of Recognition,
Torches of Greetings.
So much to talk about in seven-and-a-half minutes!
The courage of Donal McCann and what
Really it means

To be a man of faith. My God! My God!
The "Elegy for Iris" by John Bayley
In last week's *New Yorker*.
I say: "Wasn't it very touching?"
"Oh it was," Brian Friel smiles,
A sunny surmise
Lapping the steep, black cliff-face of his brow
"But I wonder if it might not have been
A wee bit *too* touching?"
"Oh Brian!"
We laugh and laugh and laugh. And laugh and laugh.
He adds gravely "Some good things here"
Lifting up from the counter and brandishing
A copy of *The Yellow Book* by Derek Mahon.

He has to hurry off to meet a Mr Colgan
To discuss a new translation of *Uncle Vanya*.
I clutch in my hands a novel by Haruki Murakami,
The Wind-up Bird Chronicle.
I say: "Everyone in Belfast's reading Haruki Murakami."
He says: "Are they? Haruki Murakami?"
What a relief to meet a northerner
Who not only has not read Haruki Murakami
But who has never heard of Haruki Murakami!
I say: "They are also reading Banana Yoshimoto."
He cries: "Look, Paul, this Mr Colgan is waiting for me."

He leaves me in the hands of a Mrs Sweeney,
A woman sailing-friend from County Donegal with
Her own white teeth, her own golden hair, her own blue
    eyes.
I turn to the Waterstone's man Cormac Kinsella and
    implore him:
"After meeting Brian Friel every twenty years
I always feel like dancing!"

Cormac Kinsella obliges as Cormac Kinsella always obliges:
"Dance away!"
I look Mrs Sweeney in the eye.
She blinks and I take her in my arms
And we begin to waltz round Waterstone's bookshop,
In and out the New Fiction shelves,
Poetry and Irish Biography.

On the Waterstone's 1920s wind-up gramophone
With His Master's Voice brass horn
Cormac Kinsella puts on a 78 of "The Blue Danube"
And I shout into Mrs Sweeney's ear:
"Is Brian Friel a grasshopper?"
"No, he is not a grasshopper.
You *scallywag* you.
Don't you know yet?
Brian Friel's a dragonfly!
And with all due respect to your parvenu feet
He's the only man in Ireland who knows how to dance."

Dancing with Brian Friel!
Who lives in that part of the South of Ireland
Which is more northerly than the North;
Who lives far away up in the South –
In the South that's far north of the North;
In County Donegal;
On the Inishowen Peninsula;
Who knows every millimetre of the road between Muff
    and Aught:
The North Road to the Deep South
By Brian Friel.

Life begins at seventy!
The all-clear of death

Being sounded far out to sea
Beyond Tory and beyond
On a single key of black ivory with one blind young lady's
   pink little finger.

The Rule of Marie Foley

At openings of art exhibitions
We stand apart, mingle,
Drift in and out caves
Of jungle shyness,
Gaze at one another,
Peer at, stand back from,
Surge close to one another,
Creatures of coral
Undulating with wineglasses
In our prehistoric claws.

On the coral beach of her art
Marie Foley has cast us:
Over eras of billions of years
Night after night
In her coastal planetarium
Marie Foley has ruled us
Until we are what we are –
Bric-a-brac of coral
Over whom ocean-profound oak trees
Lord with envious sympathy.

On the coral beach of her art
There are no I's or Me's;
On the coral beach of her art
There are only Us and Fate.
No need to gaze at me anymore.
Put your head on my shoulder.
Night's what we're born for.
Be conceived on our shore:
Dream-foetuses;
Memory-embryos.

Physicianstown, Callan, Co. Kilkenny, 30 April 1993

On this blue day in Physicianstown –
A grey day in Oslo –
Tony O'Malley –
A man with an eye for a bit of skirting board –
Scans in ragwort
A bit of skirting board,
Holds it up to his ear.

What does a bit of skirting board
Have to say to an eighty-year-old man?
What does the sea
Have to say to a boy?

My shelf is empty.
My cup is full.

I am so happy to be alone
I cannot tell you, my dearest love.
O Jane of all my days, how shall I praise
You for giving me back my loneliness or nearly?

Portrait of Winston Churchill as Seamus Heaney, 13 April 1999

to Seamus Heaney on his 60th birthday
"My soul wept in my hand"

Is there a goal in Stephen Dedalus?
There is — oh yes, there is —
There is a goal in Stephen Dedalus.

Don't stab me in the face!
Don't kiss me in the back!
Away with melancholia!
Away with black dog!
Away with the squealing of assassins
Under the oaks around the Vice-Regal Lodge!
After murders in the Phoenix Park,
Picky rain after fatty blood,
"Multitudinous seas incarnadine",
There is, Banquo, there is
Such a thing as innocence!

Come be with me in Derry
Fishing for eels,
Chaste and ignorant
As the dawn;
From tiny toe
To large intestine
A lost wax machine;
Spatula-eyed,
Damson-stubbled;

Or, if not eels, perch
On oaky banks of Bann;
Toomebride Lookout
Crouching at the weir of my easel,
Plump silver in my father's farmer's hat,
Exhaling not a loud, obese cigar
But a quiet, discreet cheroot –
A Cúl hAodh cheroot –
Spumey *sprezzatura* –
Quaffing Black Bush
From mother's silver thimble,
An about-to-be silent bee
Trowelling watercolours on grey cartridge paper.

O My Trowel Flourisher of Ithaca,
O My Sumo Wrestler of Blenheim!
O My Lord Buddha of Bellaghy!
O Bubble of Nada – Thine Empery!
Thine Shaven Posse!
Thine Cloaked Comitatus!
Boa Island Man! Gallipoli Man!
Yeats! Casement! Parnell! Tennyson!
Seamus Murphy! Saint-Gaudens!
Sam's Cross! March of the Nation!
Teilhard in Anahorish fondling
Twixt thumb and wedding finger
Stone from stream:
Not a sling stone, no:
"Always passing, the stream of life,
Which in the stream of life we trace
Is dearer than them all."

After sky wars
Severed tongues self-seeding

In wild rhubarb – pleading
"No more oaths bleeding
Between us, feeding
Cunts and *fucks*".

At the weir of our easels
We are two commas
In history crouching
Whom hawks squealing
Mistake for swallows hopping;
Our spotted tail coats mesmerize their eyes.

Wars make nothing happen.
Only the painting of poetry
Makes anything happen.
Warrior statesman as poet
Blooming at the eel weir
Of the arts of peace:
"The end of art is peace."

Is there a goal in Stephen Dedalus?
There is – oh yes, there is –
There is a goal in Stephen Dedalus.

The Pasha of Byzantium

In Thanksgiving Lar Cassidy 1950–1997

Edging past a coffee house in Baggot Street – Georgian Fare –
I spot the Literature Officer of the Arts Council in the window
Getting his priorities right:
Sipping a white cup of black coffee.
He is beaming at me.
I think: how lucky we Irish are
To have a Literature Officer who does care;
It is a hard old station
Being a Literature Officer who does care.

It is scurrying rain – a scurrying of mice feet.
I am carrying a mattress
With the help of a freckled, blond Berliner
Who is shod in glossy, red, high-heeled shoes.
Why wouldn't he be beaming at me?
I met her on the train yesterday
Trekking back up to Dublin from Mayo
And I am hoping against hope
That she is about to become my next partner.

My potential next partner – but
It was not to be – cries: "I know
What you are thinking!" I cry:
"Tell me what I am thinking – you are always right."
"You are thinking of the vision of William Butler Yeats;
That art is reality;

That to be a forty-seven-year-old Literature Officer
In Ireland you have to have all the guts –
As well as all the oil – of the Pasha of Byzantium."

13 OCTOBER 1997

The Night of the Princess

i.m. Lady Di

I used like to perch in the doorway of our bathroom
Listening to the silence:
I remember late one spring evening after my husband
In a tantrum slammed our bedroom door
And drove off to cringe on his mistress's breast
I stood there listening to the gutter dripping.
There was nowhere I felt more at home
Than in our bathroom
Eavesdropping on silence – on the gutter dripping.

I saw each drop coming out of nothing.
I put my hand over my mouth.
I could see the embryo of each drop.
I could see its rabbit nostrils beginning to form
On the lip of the gutter.
I could see it trembling in the freezing rain.
I could see its global curiosity.
I could see the tears in its eyes;
The hurt, girlish smile on its lips:

A teenage girl in a mini
In the first hour of her first job
Being a nanny in Knightsbridge, a skivvy,
Lords of the Nile tiptoeing in and out of her daydream:
In the arms of her Pharaoh
In the back seat of his car
After dinner at the Ritz –

To drive off the edge of Paris into Egypt!
Into the Pyramids, not to be gleaned ever again!

The drop drops and I switch on the bathroom light.
Switch it off. Switch it on.

Dead, Dodie, dead. Die, Di, die.

3 I AUGUST 1997

At the Funeral Mass in Tang and the Burial Afterwards in Shrule of Dr Hugh M. Drummond

I dream of my death
As a young girl dreams of her wedding –
The most important day of my life.

I

1.15 p.m. in the cafeteria at Dublin airport
Trying to prise open a prepackaged overpriced ham sandwich
On Thursday February the fifth and realizing
That most things are beyond me.

II

A week today at this very minute
February the twelfth
Instead of seeing off my daughter Síabhra flying to London
To meet up with your son Blaise
I am standing on the banks of the River Inny
Attending your funeral Mass in Tang
And the burial afterwards in Shrule.

Dr Hugh M. Drummond
In no sense could it be said that I knew you;
Yet this I know – that you were a good man
Because only a man who is good
Could have lived and worked in Liverpool
All the years of his life

To wind up in Tang and Shrule
In a house with a garden,
In a grave under a tree
On a hill overlooking a river.

I am consoled by the beating down of clay on your coffin;
The downpour of clods and spadefuls;
By the hand in the trouser pocket of the officiating priest
Giving out the rosary
While holding in the other hand the banner
MAY OUR LIVES BE ROOTED IN LOVE.

III

Back in the house – your home –
Thronged with mourners drinking and eating
My last glimpse is a glimpse
Of your son Blaise with my daughter
In the half-dark of a doorway,
A potted oak tree in his hands.

I walk away, revisit your fresh,
Filled-in, heaped-up grave;
Find you standing at the edge.
You point upstream
To a patch of sunlight on dark water
And you cry out:
"That's my son Blaise in his 'yacht'."

IV

Yes yes yes dear dead Dr Drummond!

V

In the deserted village of paradise
You stand like your own grave-digger
With your chin on the handle of your spade watching
Your son Blaise lighting up the darkness
Of the earthly world far down below;
May our lives be rooted in love
Of the earthly world far down below;
"Thou hast given him his heart's delight."

I dream of my death
As a young girl dreams of her wedding –
The most important day of my life.

Mother in April

i. m. Iris O'Neill

The little cherry tree of my life
By cancer's pinking shears
Shorn of its surface,
Its tidal blossom,
Its soul-silk.

After the service in Gilnahirk
Presbyterian Church,
After the Minister has uttered,
Good John McVeigh,
Vouched for me,
He will take down his saw,
Lop off my boughs
So that my singing-by-the-sea daughter
Will have firewood for the shores of winter.

Dearest – now that I am cut down –
Cut down – not gone –
I will keep you warm.
Bury your head in the heat of my death;
At my soul's knees glowing
I will keep you warm.

The Shankill Road Massacre,
23 October 1993

In the city of Belfast
At 2.15 p.m.
On Saturday 23 October 1993
A man in a black leather jacket
Walks into a sit-down café –
Granny's Pantry.
He orders a glass of milk,
Two plates of toasted
Ham and cheese sandwiches,
A large pot of tea.
He sits down alone near the till.

The nineteen-year-old girl behind the counter
Brings the man over his food on a tray,
Her face a surveyor's map of mirth.
She has short hair black as coal.
Cheeks red as jam.
In a red jumper and black miniskirt
She stands over him, laughing.
From head to toe, laughing.
From breasts to knees, laughing.
From elbows to eyes, laughing.
The tiered cake of her laughter
Iced with her nineteen years.

When the man in the black leather jacket
Stands up to pay her
She announces: £6.50.
He hands her a ten pound note.

He grunts at her: Keep the change.

Keep the change? £3.50?
She puts up her hands to her face
As she watches the man in the black leather jacket
Walk out of the shop.
She hides her face in her hands, weeping.

Without you my tummy is empty.
You are the sky of my tummy.

The Bloomsday Murders, 16 June 1997

> – A nation? says Bloom. A nation is the
> same people living in the same place.
> *Ulysses,* Bodley Head edition, 1960, p.489

Not even you, Gerry Adams, deserve to be murdered:
You whose friends at noon murdered my two young men,
David Johnston and John Graham;
You who in the afternoon came on TV
In a bookshop on Bloomsday signing books,
Sporting a trendy union shirt.
(We vain authors do not wear collars and ties.)

Instead of the bleeding corpses of David and John
We were treated to you gazing up into camera
In bewilderment fibbing like a spoilt child:
"Their deaths diminish us all."
You with your paterfamilias beard,
Your Fidel Castro street-cred,
Your Parnell martyr-gaze,
Your Lincoln gravitas.
O Gerry Adams, you're a wicked boy.

Only on Sunday evening in sunlight
I met David and John up the park
Patrolling the young mums with prams.
"Going to write a poem about us, Paul?"
How they laughed! How they saluted!
How they turned their backs! Their silver spines!

Had I known it, would I have told them?
That for next Sunday's newspaper I'd compose a poem

How you, Gerry Adams, not caring to see,
Saw two angels in their silver spines shot.

I am a citizen of the nation of Ireland –
The same people living in the same place.
I hope the Protestants never leave our shores.
I am a Jew and my name is Bloom.
You, Gerry Adams, do not sign books in my name.
May God forgive me – lock, stock, and barrel.

Rainy Day Doorway, Poyntzpass, 6 March 1998

A conversation from under two cars

PHILIP: Did you hear the news?

DAMIEN: I did.

PHILIP: Water on the moon!

DAMIEN: I'm going. Are you going?

PHILIP: Funny hearing the news when you're dead.

DAMIEN: I'd prefer to hear it alive.

PHILIP: So would I.

DAMIEN: Do you think they'll give us our lives back?

PHILIP: Not at all. Do you?

DAMIEN: Not at all. What'll we do?

PHILIP: Let's stay talking under our cars.

DAMIEN: Dammit, you're right. Let's stay talking under our cars.

PHILIP: If only people believed in cars the way we do.

DAMIEN: Och, people do when they're let.

PHILIP: Are you right there, my dark Damien, next Tuesday
            for an old glass on the moon?

DAMIEN: I am right there, my fair Philip, next Tuesday for
            an old glass on the moon.

North and South

At Ireland's extremities –
Malin Head in the North,
Mizen Head in the South –
Two identical notices:
PRIVATE KEEP OUT

The identical islander
At the end of his identical tether:
Dune grass, starved sheep, barbed wire;
Whitewashed, womanless cottage.
PRIVATE KEEP OUT

Politics

> In our time the destiny of man presents
> its meaning in political terms.
>
> THOMAS MANN

At the bottle bank in the shopping centre carpark
I was lobbing wine bottles into the green tank
When I saw what I thought was a human leg
Clad in trouser and boot, protruding
From under the far end of the tank.
I peered round the tank and saw
That the leg belonged to a face I recognized
Although I had not set eyes on him
For at least seventeen years.

It was the Associate Professor of Modern Irish History.
He was sitting upright on the ground
Between the tank and the hedge.
He had a white enamel toothmug in his hand
Into which he was emptying a litre can of Guinness.
There was froth on his lips and he had not shaved
For a week or two, sporting a fine, white stubble.

"Down and Out in Dublin and Paris"
He announced before I had time
To reach for words myself
"But"– he added, an erudite smile in each eye –
"Who's complaining?
I'm not!"

While I lurked above him foostering,
Shifting from one foot to the other,

He adjusted to a more
Comfortable sitting position,
Crossing his legs,
A Lord of the Animals position,
And – not taking his eyes off me –
Took out of his breast pocket his pipe
And in between swallows
Lit up scrupulously, painstakingly.

It was embarrassingly obvious that I puzzled him
As if somehow I seemed out of place.
Compassionately he stared up at me
Out of black horn-rimmed spectacles
Brushing back a forelock of his mane of grey hair.
In my jerkin and jeans I felt so commonplace
Whilst he looked so distinguished sitting down there
At 11.30 a.m. in the morning in between showers.

He delivered himself of a second pronouncement:
"The boot now is definitely on the other foot."
I stared at his grand pair of laced black boots,
His crumpled pinstripe suit, his polka-dot bow tie.
He remarked: "Not a bad carpark?"
I assented and when I could think of nothing else to say
He declared: "Recycling is catching on.
Young people like yourself are beginning
To take recycling seriously."
He sighed snotfully.

He took another deep, long, puff from the pipe
And a scoop of his stout
And folded his arms and nodded his head.
I saw satisfaction steaming out of him.
But not only satisfaction – something else also,
Something you might call tranquillity.

Or rectitude.
"The truth" he added
"The truth is that we should never have left the
        Commonwealth."

He sat up straight, looked me in the eye more steadily
With that medley of deference and defiance
That an elder in the palaeolithic would deploy
Looking down the lens of a TV camera.
And I – I in my Nike white trainers
And my Nike white baseball cap –
I felt even more commonplace.

Later, on my way back from the pharmacy,
With my little, white, pocket carrier bags
Of sleeping pills and antidepressants,
My Tranxene 7.5 and my Seroxat 20,
And my newspapers under my arms,
The *Guardian* and the *Irish Times*,
Worrying about war and war's alarms,
About Irish and Northern Irish and English politics,
I spotted him at the checkout in the supermarket,
A box of Kellogg's Special K cradled in his arms,
The teenage checkout girl listening to him rapt
To the fury of the tight, small queue behind him.
He is chatting her up!
Jail would not be half good enough for him!
Dirty old man!
Sodden sodden sodden sodden sodden!
Look at his brains! His purple brains!
Soufflé all wormy with lechery!
"Do you know you're a really pretty young woman?
You and I must try out the disco in The Hunter's Moon
Across the street from Dardis & Dunn Seeds.

Have you ever looked into Dardis & Dunn Seeds?
Compared to the 1916 Crucifixion up the road
Dardis & Dunn Seeds is appealing.
Yes. Well. You know.
The truth is that we should never have left the
    Commonwealth."

On Being Commissioned by a Nine-Year-Old Boy in Belfast to Design a Flag to Wave on the Steps of City Hall on the Twelfth of July, 1998

> Come – pledge again thy heart and hand –
> One grasp that ne'er shall sever;
> Our watchword be – "Our Native Land" –
> Our motto – "Love for ever",
> And let the Orange lily be
> Thy badge, my patriot brother –
> Thy everlasting Green for me:
> And we for one another
>
> JOHN D. FRASER, *Song for July 12th, 1843*

Dear Niall MacMichael – nine-year-old son of Harland and Wolff –
Like you, I also used cling to ships and flags, keels and stitches,
Used grip my father's hand while he compèred without
    microphones
The Plimsoll Line and the flags of the maritime nations.
I hereby present you with your new Irish flag
"The Tricolour Union Jack":
A small red, white and blue crossroads framed
By fields of green, white and orange.

May you, boy, man of the twenty-first century,
Your children, your great-grandchildren,
Under the Tricolour Union Jack
Enjoy fair weather, equal duties
And never – never – nationalism or imperialism:
Those sucking ideologies of self-pity!
Long live the Republic! Long live the Union!

8 a.m. News, Twelfth of July 1998

i.m. Richard (10), Mark (9) and Jason (7) Quinn

"Adams Calls For Calm";
"Archbishop Cannot Find Words";
"Paisley Commiserates On Murdered Children".

O God, why was I ever born?
Why cannot our Three Wise Musketeers
Instead of shooting the crap *en suite* –
Instead of locking themselves into
Their private lavatories,
Take tea together at Drumcree,
Hold hands, and
For the first time
In northwest European histor-ee
Move their bowels together?
Their gold-as-sunset bowels?
We poor Irish could do with a little
Excremental togetherness.

And God – what of Poor Old God?
Still young at heart, tramping the galaxies,
On the northwest seashore of northwest Europe
God picks up an orangey-greeny stone, peruses it,
Sobs to himself – *"Got Ireland here"* –
Spits on it, and over-arm
Bowls it into the bored-stiff ocean.
Ask my Granny – God weeps – *ask my Granny.*

The Voice of Eden

for Colm on your eleventh birthday

Playing golf aged eleven
In Ballybunnion in the rain;
Playing a seven iron and not being able
To see the hole and pitching up
Pin high! *Pin high!*
Seeking to emulate my father –
His swing, his sexy swing,
His Christy O'Connor slouch;
Trudging after him into nightfall.

After our game
Instead of driving home
He drives up on to the cliff,
Parks the black Vauxhall Wyvern
At right angles to the castle wall
About to subside into the Atlantic ocean;
His front wheels on the cliff edge;
His headlights switched on high beam –
Spotlights on the spouting, snorting nostrils of the sea.

For what are we waiting here?
I dare not enquire.
I am scared.
I am thrilled.
Is he watching out for ships?
For smugglers, gunrunners?
For that giant in history whom he pines for –
Roger Casement?

From under the driver's seat
He plucks a transistor radio
Cuddling it in his lap,
Coaxing out of its knobs
The BBC Home Service.

In the night in the rain
Through static
Like two silhouetted
Samurai in a canoe
On the brink of a thirty-foot wave
We listen to the voice of Eden
Trot across the ocean,
Black hooves shod in silver:
"I have to tell you that we are on the brink
Of a crisis grave as World War II.
By his criminal annexation of the Suez Canal
Colonel Nasser seeks to emulate
Hitler's annexation of Czechoslovakia.
Her Majesty's Government is at war with Egypt."

We crouch in silence, Daddy and I,
A pair of fugitives,
Creatures of euphoria
And of blame,
Appalled,
Enchanted by
The voice of Eden
In Ballybunnion in the rain.

30 MAY 1997

56 Ken Saro-Wiwa Park

Having heard this morning's news of the hanging of Ken
    Saro-Wiwa
With eight comrades in the state prison in Port Harcourt
I drove immediately to the Nigerian Embassy at 56 Leeson Park,
    Dublin 6.
I expected to find the Embassy cordoned off by police,
The gates locked, the curtains drawn and, in my confusion
    and shock,
The Nigerian flag to be flying at half-mast.

Instead, the gates were open, the curtains were open,
And there was not one single Irish policeman in sight.
There was no one nor nothing to be seen in Leeson Park
Except in the gutter a black, bloody ooze of leaves.
There were only gyrating crimson leaves on quartz, granite steps;
Ogoni bannerettes gyrating in wind and rain on stone.

As I stood alone in the gutter, ankle-deep in the crimson ooze,
Gazing up at the squeaky-clean sash window
I began to realize I could discern a face in that glassy black limbo –
A bejewelled, black face fanning itself with a white shell fan –
Her Excellency the Ambassador gazing back out the window
    lasciviously
At the sedate, autumnal tranquillity of this leafy Dublin city
    suburban morning.

How nice to be in Ireland this slightly irritating morning.
How nice to be in Leeson Park with gravel paths, palinged lawns.
How residential, opulent, decorous Leeson Park is.
How nice the Irish are this slightly irritating morning.

Look me in the eye, Madam Ambassador.
Listen to the renaming of Leeson Park.
Because of your murdering hate
Leeson Park can never again be Leeson Park.
I am now standing, you are now sitting
In Ken Saro-Wiwa Park.
Madam Ambassador, get out your new headed fax paper:

Her Excellency Mrs N. U. O. Wadibia-Anyanwu,
Embassy of the Federal Republic of Nigeria,
56 Ken Saro-Wiwa Park,
Dublin 6.

11 NOVEMBER 1995

Mohangi's Island

Me and Mohangi were sitting over a pot of tea
In the lobby of the Hilton in Mogadishu.
Mohangi said to me: How are things in Tír na nÓg?
I said to Mohangi: Things ain't good in Tír na nÓg.
Mohangi said: What do you mean – things ain't good in
    Tír na nÓg?
I said: The young are getting old in Tír na nÓg.
Mohangi said: I'm going into islands.
I said: Glad to hear you're going into islands, Mohangi.
Mohangi said: There's an island north of Europe.
I said: An island north of Europe? Sounds cool.
Mohangi said: If I buy, will you manage?
I said: What's in it for me, Mohangi?
Mohangi said: Grass, seaweed, treebark.
I said: But, Mohangi, you know that what I like best to do in
    life is to judge – to do lots and lots and lots of judging.
Mohangi said: Oh – there'll be a whole lot of judging going on.
I said: Oh, Mohangi, I would like to judge and judge and judge –
    and judge and judge and judge and – judge and judge
    and judge and judge and judge and judge and judge
    and judge and judge and judge and judge and judge.
Mohangi said: You could judge till the cows come home.
I said: And drop live cows out of airplanes?
Mohangi said: And drop live cows out of airplanes.
I said: We have lift off, Mohangi.
Mohangi said: Take her up, Durcan, take her up.

All my best friends are dying in Mohangi's Island,
All sitting at home in their houses dying.
But I – I am flying low over Mohangi's Island
Dropping cows on my best friends' houses.

Letter to the Archbishop
of Cashel and Emly

Dear Archbishop Dermot – I am a divorced man
And, therefore, as you so charitably preach,
Seven times more likely to tell lies
Than a married man.
I tell a lie to begin with!
Although my marriage ended twelve years ago
I am *not* divorced because I live in Rathvegas in Cashel,
Not far from Ballyreno in Emly.
Liar that I am, it is nevertheless true to say
That when I was married
I smoked like a train and I drank like a tank
But since my marriage ended
I neither smoke nor drink.
When I was married
Although I didn't know how to drive a car
I was involved in a car accident
(No firstclass tickets to Florida for guessing who was driving!)
But since my marriage ended
I have learned to drive a car
And – you will be mortified to hear –
I have been involved in no accidents.
When I was married
I looked on the dark side of suicide
But since my marriage ended
I look on the bright side of suicide.
Unfortunately – you will be mortified again –
I appear to be very much alive
So much so that I have a lover
With whom I live in sin

Which I enjoy enormously
But which I'd enjoy more
If it was married sin
And whose grown-up daughters
I do not abuse nor they me.

Sordid, Dermot, sordid
Statistics of a separated spouse.
What is to be done?
While you were preaching compassion in Holy Cross
Michelle Smith was winning the butterfly in Vienna.
Let's ask her to preach to us in Holy Cross
The stroke of compassion.
Let's enter you – truth-addicted Archbishop Dermot –
In next Sunday's women's 200-metre butterfly,
Tog you out in black bikini becoming to your statistics
With purple skullcap and goldrimmed goggles
And watch you pound the pool –
Pure spirit, pure bubbles, not a squeak of flesh.
Yours faithfully, Paul "Marry the Sinner" Durcan.

AUGUST 1994

A Nineties Scapegoat Tramping
at Sunrise

I

A nineties scapegoat tramping at sunrise
I arrive at a five-barred gate on Achill Island –
The last island of Europe before Newfoundland waters –
To find two agèd neighbours either side of it chatting.
On this side of the gate – Charles Haughey;
On the far side of the gate – Bishop Eamonn Casey.

Bishop Casey – a straying Irish Catholic –
Finding homes for the homeless in London
Had the habit of saying "*How* are you?"
With all the stress on *how*.

Charles Haughey – a straying Irish politician –
Used raise money for artists, the agèd and children
Had also the habit of saying "*How* are you?"
With all the stress on *how*.

II

And you? What did you do?
And for whom did you do it?
Did you do it for the love of God?
Or for the love of yourself?

You wrote poetry – is that what you did?
For fame, was it? You're not serious!

III

How are you, Charlie?
How are you, Eamonn?
Things could be worse, Charlie.
Things could be worse, Eamonn.

IV

A nineties scapegoat tramping at sunrise
I clamber over the gate
Into the next acre, into the next century,
On, on towards Equality!

Dropping down onto my knee, glancing up over my
    shoulder,
I see that bush of prickly gold
Irishmen call "furze".
I kiss her on the mountain and close my eyes.

Omagh

1. From the Omagh Quartermaster: Memo to GHQ, 16.08.98

Gerry, *a chara*, I am vexed with you.
I have every right to be vexed with you.
I am referring to your "unequivocal condemnation".
Lucky for you, you did not go any further.
I was *terrified* – always a man for the pun – *terrified*
You might sound off about the "sanctity of life"
Or that you might start apologizing for the past
And say something really stupid like "I'm sorry".
What is the matter with you, Gerry?
When I did the very same thing in Jerusalem
(Those two overcrowded buses, d'ye nae remember?)
There was not an *ochón* out of you.
You're a terrible man when it comes to the truth about terror.
You and your boys need to cop yourselves on.
We were in it with the ANC, and HAMAS
From the start, and we are not copping out now.
What I would like to know is:
Are you seriously proposing that Omagh
Is a different kettle of fish to Canary Wharf?
By the way, remember the name of the Paki
We topped at Canary? For the life of me, I cannot.
(In my next seminar in Libya on terror –
Remember singing "Kevin Barry" in Irish in the Colonel's tent? –
I must remember to tell the Libos
That massacring people is bad for the memory.
The more you kill, the less you remember.)

Okay, it was a balls-up in Omagh.
But in the past we've had many balls-ups
And we learnt long ago not to be cry-babies
And to blame it always on the Brits and their agents,
Their stooges and stool pigeons.
The republican family is a family –
Not a bloody orphanage.
We've been in terror for thirty years, Gerry.
Or are you telling me that you're an ex-terrorist?
There is no such thing as an ex-terrorist
And well you, above all, know it.
Terror is terror that has no end.

Here we are, Gerry. What about the next Omagh?
And the next Canary Wharf?
What about all the Omaghs down the road?
For every Good Friday
There has to be a Feast of the Assumption.
A terrible beauty
Was never, is never, and never will be born.
Come on, pop the propaganda and face up
To all the Omaghs and Canarys of the future.
Terror is terror that has no end.

Tell you what.
You stick to the word games – to all the palaver,
All the mantras: "The politics of the next atrocity".
"The atrocity of the last politics", etc., etc.,
(By the way, congratulations on "dissident republican" –
A grand wee contradiction in terms.
How about a bit of "progressing pacifism"
Or "moving pacifism forward"?)
Enjoy the rest of your holidays.
In spite of everything we still need boys like yourself
Who can sing in Irish and influence people.

Leave the real talking to us – we
Who are the real *óglaigh*, Beir bua. The Quartermaster.

2. *Le Monde*

In tomorrow's *Le Monde* there was
a reprint of Robespierre's essay
"On the Theory and Function of Terror in History".

3. *First Litany*

Omagh
Omagh
Carrickmore
Buncrana
Buncrana
Buncrana
Madrid
Madrid
Drumquin
Beragh
Aughadarra
Aughadarra
Aughadarra
Aughadarra
Beragh
Omagh
Omagh
Gortaclare
Omagh
Omagh
Newtownsville

Omagh
Omagh
Carrickmore
Omagh
Omagh
Omagh
Omagh
Omagh
Omagh
Omagh

4. *Second Litany*

Breda Devine
Julie Hughes
Brenda Logue
James Barker
Oran Doherty
Sean McLaughlin
Fernando Blasco
Rocio Abad
Philomena Skelton
Esther Gibson
Avril Monaghan
Maura Monaghan
Unborn twin baby Monaghan
Unborn twin baby Monaghan
Mary Grimes
Geraldine Breslin
Anne McCombe
Veda Short
Aidan Gallagher
Elizabeth Rush
Jolene Marlow

Samantha McFarland
Lorraine Wilson
Gareth Conway
Alan Radford
Fred White
Brian White
Brian McCrory
Olive Hawkes
Deborah Anne Cartwright
Sean McGrath

5. *Third Litany*

Aged twenty months
Aged twenty-one years
Aged seventeen years
Aged twelve years
Aged eight years
Aged twelve years
Aged twelve years
Aged twenty-four years
Aged thirty-nine years
Aged thirty-six years
Aged thirty years
Aged eighteen months
Aged minus one month
Aged minus one month
Aged sixty-five years
Aged thirty-five years
Aged forty-eight years
Aged forty-six years
Aged twenty-one years
Aged fifty-seven years
Aged seventeen years

Aged seventeen years
Aged fifteen years
Aged eighteen years
Aged sixteen years
Aged sixty years
Aged twenty-seven years
Aged fifty-four years
Aged sixty years
Aged twenty years
Aged sixty-one years

6. *After the Remembrance Is Over*

Seven days and seven nights
And twenty minutes after the massacre
It is half past the hour of three o'clock
On Saturday afternoon in the town of
    Omagh.
The Act of Remembrance is over.
What are we to do now,
O People of Sion?
O People of Tyrone
Where will I go?
To the hills?
To Ben's Bar?
Or back to my room?
I ask you.
What? Where? With whom?

7. *Efforts of Conversation*

What do you make of Omagh?
Roma?
No, Omagh?
Oh, OMAGH!

8. *Sunday the Twenty-third of August*

Blinking in Omagh.

9. *What Ben Says*

Do not talk to me of "death
Giving birth to life".
Do not talk to me
Of "post-trauma management".
Do not talk to me.

10. *Ben Again*

If you want to give me something –
Really give me something real –
Give me the allegiance of your silence.
Man to man, Ben to Ben:
Never to have to speak again.

11. *Tall Ships*

Towards the end of the twentieth century,
Four days after the Omagh Massacre,
While the funerals were steaming
The Three Rivers of Omagh
To and from the Black Bog,
The Tall Ships Race berthed in Dublin:
Mir of St Petersburg,
Libertad of the Armada Argentina,
Sir Winston Churchill of the United Kingdom.
Old Dublin men, old Dublin women cried:
The happiest civic event of the century!
On cobble stones, a million children shone.

12. *Letter to Ben, 22 August 1998*

There is no such thing
As eternity.
There is no such thing
As the "eternal reciprocity of tears".
In Omagh of the Blackbirds
Nonreciprocal are the tears
Of a murdered daughter's father.
In this summer of rain, my closest grief
Lies in Tyrone dust. There is no man
Who would not murder his brother.
So, in history, the ridge becomes deserted now
    and then:
Right now, just you and me, Ben, and the species.

13. *The Wednesday after the Wednesday after the Saturday*

I stand in my doorway in the sun at noon.
Paul Francis Durcan at home in Ringsend.
The Wednesday after the Wednesday after the Saturday.
Wednesday. Bin collection day –
Until this week. Last week
I received a notice from Dublin Corporation
Cleaning Division, 66/71 Marrowbone Lane:
"As from next week your weekly Collection will take
    place on a Tuesday.
Any inconvenience this change may cause is regretted."

Standing in my doorway wondering if the post has come.
My doctor posted my prescription for antidepressants
And sleeping pills three days ago.
The avenue is empty, pink under blue skies.
A '97 red Volkswagen Polo drives in –
My friendly neighbour Bernie. I notice
Four black plastic bulging refuse sacks
Most neatly stacked under her windowsill.
I ask her if she got post today.
"Oh yes I did, Paul, he came early today."
I attempt to conceal my bowel-puncturing anxiety.
I ask her if she received the Corporation notice.
"Oh Lord I did but I forgot all about it.
Jim will kill me!
Oh well, it's not the end of the world."

I go back inside my den and phone
The local Postal Delivery Office.
No sign there of my missing precription.
A quiet-voiced, slowly spoken man murmurs:
"These things happen, unfortunately.

I put the phone down and place
My two hands flat on the desk.
Calm down, Paul, calm down.
Listen to the broad hum of the city.
Dublin is a broad city and you are part of it.
How lucky you are to be part of it.
As lucky as the people of Lisbon
Are to be part of Lisbon.
Pray *to*, as well as *for*,
The people of Omagh.
You who have water, gas, electricity,
The kindest of neighbours.
You who are sated with tranquillity,
Brimming with sufficiency.
Books, paper, pens.
Fruit, bread, milk.
Pray *for*, *to*, the people of Omagh.
Omagh have mercy on me.

14. *The Last Post*

No, I cannot forgive you.
For the extinction of the moans –
Unborn, born –
Of children's cries in Omagh,
Of wives' cries in Omagh,
Of husbands' cries in Omagh,
Of students' cries in Omagh,
Of the cries of single women in Omagh,
Of the cries of single men in Omagh,
I cannot forgive you.

On the Morning of Christ's Nativity

to Michael Mullen

It is Christmas Night, I am eighteen years old,
Moseying the streets of Dublin city;
On O'Connell Street Bridge in my military greatcoat,
My little destiny inside me lurking to be born;
Am I Collins? Am I Connolly? Am I Che Guevara?
I can feel the fear upside-down in my stomach.

Moseying the Christmas lights of my native city:
Eden Quay, Mary Street, Henry Street, Moore Street;
Merchant's Arch, Harry Street, Wicklow Street, Duke Street;
The last street-vendors scampering off behind the last
      wheelbarrows;
The pubs gleaming at the seams with the extended family
      of man;
Harry Kernoff, Thérèse Cronin, Bob Bradshaw, all the team.
Why on earth did God make man?
To slay the dry dragon of scaly spite;
To give birth to the red wine of peace on the streets.

In the arrogance of my adolescence
I have renounced wine, women and song;
I linger on O'Connell Street Bridge
Dallying with reflections of an oozy death;
The old river says no;
My middle-aged, storytelling father is caressing his bodhrán:
"O'Connell Street Bridge is as wide as it is long."

Shy, haughty, hurting
I elect to walk the gauntlet of Davy Byrne's bar;

"A throw of the dice never abolishes chance."
Diving sideways through the rout
I hear my name being called out;
My first love – a smiler with dyed yellow hair –
Cheek by cheek with Dublin's coolest bodhrán player.

At closing-time they invite me to go with them
On the proviso that they blindfold me in the taxi;
Their backstreet rented den is their secret altar.
After a gallon of red wine, they bid me good night,
Hand in hand twirl upstairs to bed.
I step outside to catch snow on my cheeks,
Sail my shoes through its cakiness.
Not only my belly
But my cheeks and my forehead as well as my feet are pregnant.

I step back inside, put more briquettes on the fire,
Stretch out on the divan with the only book in the room –
The Dharma Bums by Jack Kerouac.
Through the high, mountainy hours of Christmas Night
The Christ inside me slaloms his tiny canoe
Out into the open sea
"While birds of calm sit brooding on the charmèd wave".
Peace halcyon peace.

At 7.30 a.m. as dawn cracks
I trek home to my parents
Through the muffled-by-mittens applause
 Of the sleet-negligéed streets of Dublin city;
Up Whitefriars Street, across Charlemont Bridge;
The canal is a crow in snow.

In 57 Dartmouth Square
As I tiptoe up to my bedroom over the hall door
My parents whisper past me

On the stairs like monks
Going to eight o'clock mass.
I go to sleep in my greatcoat;
The Lamb of God in my arms.
The Christ of the Possibility
Of Family Peace bleats!

Sunday Mass, Belfast, 13 August 1995

It was during the prayers after Communion –
A woman marathon runner
Appeared around the top left-hand corner of the aisle
Having apparently raced through the sacristy
And she came running on down,
Not in the centre but not hugging the side either,
Black top, black shorts,
Yellow hair tied up in a black scrunchie.

I was seated on the aisle.
When I caught her eye
I thought she'd be embarrassed
But she was not embarrassed.
When I turned around guiltily
To steal a last glimpse of her
She had turned around at the back of the church
And she was running back up the aisle,
A winning smile on her lips, her eyes shut,
And she was flying –
Flying straight into the doors of the tabernacle –
When above the gates of the altar rail
She stalled in midair:
Her wrists flapping at the tail-ends of her arms –
Her head lolling on her shoulder –
Her knees bent –
Her two small, blue-and-white feet
In black spikes
Twined round each other.
After twenty-six years

Crossing the finishing-line;
A communicant all the way;
A dead woman.

The Mass is ended. Go in peace
To love and serve the Lady.

Self-Portrait as an Irish Jew

I

This is the letter, Mam, I dare not write;
Ear-marked to die in the desert at Alamein;
Affrighted by my fright;
His Majesty's sober soldiery burnt alive
In tanks from which there is no escape.
Tell Rabbi Robinson I kiss his beard
Despite all soupstains.
The names of his books help keep me sane.
I swear by Jove if I get home alive
To the sheep farm on the mountain behind Tallaght
I will stop on our hill top, watch the city glow-grow;
"Just those kinds of intimate things".

II

That I do swear – my fantasy, my prayer;
Save nights with my wife at the Stella Cinema
To see Spencer Tracy and his Katherine Hepburn.
I will construct my own bookshelves,
Lectern, table, chair, abacus;
Relearn to read, decipher, even pray
By the light of the bog-oak menorah.
I will read Hone's *Life of George Moore* in bed,
Relearn also how to fall asleep reading –
That phenomenal spectacle of the butterfly page
Trembling off the bevelled edge of the world;
"Just those kinds of intimate things".

III

Stop shelling stop! I hop
Out. Watch myself skip a hornpipe
That I am still alive, still alive!
Ecstatic to be a Joyce, a Ryan's man!
I salute my mate, jitterbug, swear again
And waddle off into our next affray;
Drakes into débâcle.
I can feel the desert dirt lace sand round me,
Its moisture adhering to my cheeks, my chin,
Each grain establishing a hide in my stubble;
If you could see me, Mam, you'd see my eyes;
"Just those kinds of intimate things".

Travel Anguish

A stranger in Belfast,
Alone in the universe,
I am a child astride my mother's shoulder.

In the arrivals hall of David Ben Gurion Airport in Tel Aviv
A little old man in a flaming temper
Is leaping up and down at the hatch of the carousel
Exhorting his baggage to appear.

Despite the solicitous, fraternal warnings of baggage handlers
And of fellow travellers including myself –
(The nerve of me!
I who am always frantic about my baggage!)
The little old man plunges his fingers into the flames –
Into the swaying black drapes of the baggage ovens,
Snatching at bags.

But then when the little old man attempts to climb into the
      baggage oven
A youthful rabbi with babe in arms
Who is gazing into the calm, azure eyes of his own smiling wife
Hands over the infant to his wife
And puts his two arms around the little old man, in a loving lock.

The baby howls but when the little old man's attaché case
      materializes
And he lifts it up, hugging it, embracing it, feeding it,
The baby smiles and we all stand around and watch
The little old man skip about with his attaché case in his arms,

His newborn babe delivered at last from the flames
In the midst of all these multitudes and signs.

Under the night sky outside the arrivals hall
We are confronted by crowds behind a high wire fence,
Millions of screaming faces in the night clinging to the wire.
I try to turn back but the little old man prods me forward,
Roaring into my ear: "The important thing is to get out."

Outside the wire,
On the perimeter of the screaming crowd,
He urinates into the grass,
Patriarchal piss.
He is all overcoat lapels,
Giving his breast to the universe,
Repeating his message to me:
"The important thing is to get out."

Pointing me in the direction of the Jerusalem bus,
And buttoning up his fly,
He puts his two hands up to his star-shaped lapels,
And twirling his two wrists round his breasts,
Lays his head on his left shoulder, and sideways bows to me.
I take my leave of him, bold for my journey.

A stranger in the Holy Land,
Alone in the universe,
I am a child astride my mother's shoulder.

Waiting for a Toothbrush
to Fall out of the Sky

to Juan Enrique Bécquer

I was flying from New York to Caracas – Swissair.
At the carousel in Caracas
I lounged like a vulture with my fellow carrion
Inspecting the crotchety belt ratcheting around.

I was expecting, as always presuming,
The routine miracle to occur –
That my suitcase with its dainty identity tag
Would emerge crawling out of the roomy womb
As it has done at most other airports in the world.

I found myself perched alone at the carousel
An half an hour later swooping about,
Refusing to believe that my suitcase had not appeared;
That my suitcase would not be revealed today.
Yet another curly, grey, male paragon
Taking Nature's Apparatus for granted.

Venezuelan police officers escorted me
Into a security tank to interrogate me.
I was wearing my Brazilian football team shirt
Presented to me by Socrates in Brasilia '95.

"Who are you?
Where do you come from?
Where are you going?"

"My name is Paul Durcan."
"Goggin?"
"Durcan – Irish poet."
"Irish poet?
Next you say
You are Brazilian footballer!"

Two months later Swissair fax me to say
That on the day I flew to Caracas from NY
There was also a Swissair flight to Karachi:
"Pakistan – it is not a small country, sir."

I have spent my life – not all of it a lie –
Waiting for a toothbrush to fall out of the sky.

Making Love *inside* Áras An Uachtaráin

When visitors flew into Dublin in the nineties
The first place – the only place –
I brought them to was Áras an Uachtaráin.

Dark Sunday mornings, empty streets,
I picked up visitors from hotels on the canals;
Drove down the quays up through the Phoenix Park.

The Phoenix Park which in the record books
Is one of the seven spectacles of Europe:
The largest, greenest, city park in Europe.

The ballroom throngs of chestnut trees parted.
Pulled on the ropes of their dark, green curtains
To reveal the white, Newgrange-like facade of the Áras.

At the left of the upper storey of its portico
The light in the kitchen window
Not only to the future of the unknown citizen

But to the actuality of the unknown exile
Whether he or she be a bus driver in Cleveland
Or drilling for water in North-East Brazil.

We sit in the front seats of the car in silence
Listening to the north wind gusting in the trees.
In Sunday morning dark an Ohian woman asks:

Are not the facade at Newgrange with its solar orifice
And the facade of the Áras with its light in the window
The same website – interglacial poetry?

Instead of making love *outside* Áras an Uachtaráin
We are making love *inside* Áras an Uachtaráin.
Power is conditional on love. Acton!

II

Driving into Achill Island, I am coming
Into Gowlawaum – "The Clitoris of the Gap";
Climbing up through darkness to gaze down on light –
The fire of the sea on the faces of island children.

God knows it is not possible to justify anything
Except the freedom of children to make a home on earth
In the face of death. To thrive at home
Under the rain clouds, in fidelity and tenderness.

To be utterly public is to be utterly private.
To build our own home together with our own hands.
To watch and to listen and to welcome visitors.
To do our best by our children.

Making love *inside* Áras and Uachtaráin
On the shores of Achill Island facing Newfoundland
I behold the changing face of my beloved;
As she grows older, her face grows younger.

Until she dies and goes away, far off, near,
To dwell under the star on the mountain:
My young bride with whom I have lived seven year
Making love *inside* Áras An Uachtaráin.

What did I hear you say?
Gowlawaum!
Will I hear you say it again?
Gowlawaum!

Real Inishowen Girl

to Dr Aubrey Bourke

I'll be ten in September.
She's real Inishowen girl.

When I go out playing with Tessa,
Chasing, leaping after her
Across ditches, dung,
I'm in stitches keeping up with her.
I always get stung.

I'll be ten in September.
She's real Inishowen girl.

She pretends to get cross
When I get stung
But she likes the chance to be boss.
She snags clumps of docks,
She scours my flesh.

I'll be ten in September.
She's real Inishowen girl.

I like her when she's cross with me.
Secretly she's proud of me,
Proud of my stings.
Her eyes are ice lollipops.
Her freckles are biscuits.

228

I'll be ten in September.
She's real Inishowen girl.

Her favourite game is "Souls-and-Bodies".
She hides behind the Carndonagh Cross.
All I see of her is her arms
And the palms of her hands.
The rest of her is all Cross.

I'll be ten in September.
She's real Inishowen girl.

Concealed in the Cross, she cries
"I'm dead, catch me."
All I can see of her is her soul.
I know the outside of her soul
Like the palm of my hand.

I'll be ten in September.
She's real Inishowen girl.

When I die, I know
I will go to heaven or hell.
But how can I go to heaven
When I am already in heaven?
Tessa O'Donnell is heaven.

I'll be ten in September.
She's real Inishowen girl.

Handball

I am the only girl
In a family of seven:
Four Biggles brothers
And two black cats,
Emmet and Victoria,
Sphinxes to us all.

How many hours
After flying lessons
I have spent down at the wall,
Solo in the alley
Whipping the ball!
Blue Mayo skies
Trailing rights and wrongs
In balls of wool clouds.

Each hour an eternity –
Engrossed eternities
An only girl can know
Whipping the ball
In a canary yellow T-shirt
And blue jeans.
I was the first girl
In Mayo
To wear blue jeans.

To this day
Forty-five years later
I prefer jeans and T-shirts
To blouses and skirts.

Today is my day off –
Handball in Geneva!
Chucks away!

In my jeans
I feel *gemütlich*;
Down at the wall
Solo in the alley
Whipping the ball,
Blue Swiss skies
Trailing rights and wrongs
In balls of wool clouds.

Enniscrone, 1955

to Eoghan Harris

At Enniscrone where the sea enters the river
We bought ice-cream cones and watched the races:
While the Mayo whites built petulant bungalows on the cliffs
The Mayo blacks sat homeless on the strands far down below
Chanting their Paul Robeson lullabies:
"God's going to give you a new home, down in Enniscrone."

The difference between Alabama blacks and Mayo blacks
Was that Mayo blacks did not have the advantage
Of having black faces.
Walking the strands at Enniscrone, 1955,
Mayo blacks had white faces.
Being a Mayo black in 1955
Meant rain, alcohol, emigration;
Carcasses of Volkswagen Beetles
Wax-pink on lime-green rocks.

Aged eleven years staring out to sea
I analysed the facial structure of each wave;
The teeth they grew up into – milk-white;
The cheekbones they grew up into – curvilinear;
I gaped into the beseeching mouths of waves
Until they'd collapsed at my feet:
Foam-chewing infants without energy to whimper;
Their blue mothers wreathing my shins in seaweed.

Aghast, agog at the river-entering sea
I stared through a glass pane of my father's bookcase;

At spines of volumes 1–3 of Blackwell's *Cancers of the Breast*
And Dostoyevsky's *Crime and Punishment* in the Everyman
    edition
Translated by David Magarshack. Enniscrone was
    St Petersburg –
A delta of dune-mantilla'd islands surfing the Neva and the
    Moy –
And as I scoured the shacks of the Mayo blacks
Many was the monkey-faced Pushkin stared back at me.

At Enniscrone where the sea enters the river
We bought ice-cream cones and watched the races:
While the Mayo whites built petulant bungalows on the cliffs
The Mayo blacks sat homeless on the strands far down below
Chanting their Paul Robeson lullabies:
"God's going to give you a new home, down in Enniscrone."

Private Luncheon, Maynooth Seminary, 8 July 1990

On a Sunday afternoon bored out of its own mind,
Raindrops in puddles on black leaves of chestnut trees,
In the ninth week of Mary Robinson's election campaign,
In a high-ceilinged, windowless, dado'd chamber
Waxy in the cloisters of Maynooth Seminary,
Eleven of us sat down to private luncheon.
For almost all of the two-and-a-half hours
Garret FitzGerald — gruff, pedigree statesman —
Lectured us on how Mary Robinson
Had flawed notions of the role of the presidency.
The candidate herself, sitting opposite Garret,
Scarcely uttered throughout the meal.
Twice I thought she would break down into tears
Or throw up. In a drizzle of civility
She was teetering off the edge of the world.
By luncheon's end she was sitting far out on the edge of her chair,
Baked Alaska virgin on her plate,
Her face ice-cream-white, scorched, dripping,
Her two feet in strangleholds around the legs of her chair.
Girl in a force-nine gale, on a hiding to nothing.

Edenderry

Kate drove me to Edenderry
On 25 February '92
To be at the Public Library at 11 a.m.
To give a poetry reading
To the Edenderry Women's Association.

Before or since, I have never read
At a more well-organized reading.
Afterwards, I said to Kate:
Kate, women are different from men.
Yes, Paul, women are feminine.

I sat in silence, taking her in,
Sipping my soda-and-lime.
She said: Come on,
We're here, let's sip
At the source of the Boyne.

That night in Trinity College Dublin
Mary Robinson in her Allen Lane lecture
Drew the attention of her audience
To – as she put it – the way women *organize*
Things in a fundamentally different fashion.

Edenderry is the source of the Boyne:
Spawning fields of the Boyne salmon –
The salmon of wisdom.
Ireland is not our verifiable name.
Our verifiable name is Edenderry.

The First and Last Commandment
of the Commander-in-Chief

By 1990 in Ireland we'd been adolescents for seventy years
Obsessed with the Virgin, automobiles, alcohol, *Playboy*, Unity.
The Commander-in-Chief issued her first and only
    commandment:
First and last you must learn to love your different self.

Somalia, October 1992

Are you going to throw that pothole filler a coin?
Are you going to throw that pothole filler a coin?
Are you going to throw that pothole filler a coin?
I'm going to cry my eyes out, if that poor boy dies.

Why did you apologize for your tears?
Do not ever again apologize for your tears.
You, our President, of whom we are earlobe-tinglingly proud.
Our dearest daughter of whom we bashfully boast.
What other Head of State's in tears
To throw that pothole filler a coin?

So stately, so shy :
Your barrister's foxy intelligence;
Your girl–next-door's infuriating routines.
By weeping before the television cameras of the world in
    Nairobi
After Baidoa;
After Afgoi;
After Mogadishu;
After Mandera;
You apprised the automobile-addicted, hard-porn world
That there was at least one fox in power
Whose tail was not made of plastic.

While the nineties clocked in and clocked out
You never ceased
To go down to the well;
To yoke on your neck
The dumbbell of thirst;

To hump on your shoulders
Your own two buckets of water.
You never ceased to carry on your back
The starving infant whom the world forgot.

Are you going to throw that pothole filler a coin?
Are you going to throw that pothole filler a coin?
Are you going to throw that pothole filler a coin?
I'm going to cry my eyes out, if that poor boy dies.

Meeting the President
(31 August 1995)

I

Driving up to the Phoenix Park
For a meeting with the President
On the last day of August
My father – eight years dead –
Steals my place;
Shoulders me aside;
Playfully, crudely.

I do not try to stop him
But even if I did try to stop him
It would make no difference.
As I get older, my dead father gets younger.
My hands on the driving wheel are my father's hands.
My shoulders in the driving seat are my father's shoulders.

II

I get out of bed. I shave with soap and water.
I go back to bed with my breakfast tray –
A pot of tea with no milk or sugar.
I get back out of bed at nine a.m., go downstairs
To my daughter. "Do I look respectable?"
She – cross-legged on the couch with the Koran –
She is a week back from Marrakesh –
Reassures me that I look respectable.
Black shirt, green jacket, black slacks, black shoes.

I take a sideways glance at myself in the mirror,
Behold my father's face peering out at me,
Eyebrow antler-hairs curling down into his eyes,
Jawbone flecked with ice.
He steps out the door of my one-up and one-down,
Switches off the car alarm – two blank beeps,
Lowers himself down into the driving seat, performs a u-turn
In the redbrick cul-de-sac, turns out onto the Pigeon House
    Road.
He drives slowly upriver to the Phoenix Park.

III

Riding upriver across the city of Dublin
Is for my father the most sensual of rides.
Every street name is an enigma of consolation.
It is a straight line from Ringsend to the Phoenix Park,
Only the street name changing itself every half-mile:
Ringsend Road, Pearse Street, College Street, Westmoreland
    Street;
Aston Quay, Wood Quay, Usher's Island, Parkgate Street.
He takes each fence in his stride;
One hand on the reins,
The other hand between his thighs.

At the Phoenix Park gates
He checks his watch. 10.05.
He stops at the Wellington Monument, gets out.
"The Duke of Wellington was Irish,"
He used muse to us children. "Trim!"
Clasping the obelisk to his breast, kissing the plinth,
He gazes upon all these flights of steps
To which as a Judge of the Circuit Court
He is dedicating his life,
All these myriads of treads and raisers.

At 10.12 he drives off again and takes a right turn
In between the Polo Grounds and the Zoological Gardens
Arriving at the east gate of Áras an Uachtaráin
At 10.16. It is all locked up, no sign of life.
Surprised by himself, he does not panic.
At the west gate he gets out of the car,
Peers through more locked gates. A young garda
Opens the door of the gate lodge, scratches the back of his
    head
Under his peaked cap, calls out Good Morning.
My father is in his element:
This all appears to be happening in the middle of Dublin city;
Musically it is all happening to the tune of County Mayo.
My father says: What part of the country are you from?
The guard says: I'm not from County Mayo.
My father says: What do you mean by that?
The garda smiles: Every garda in Ireland is from Mayo –
    except me.

IV

My father drives up the avenue under oak and beech.
An army officer is standing bareheaded in the doorway
Waiting to escort him.
"Commandant Lester Costelloe.
The President will be with you in six minutes.
She will come in through the door by the window.
She will sit down at the end of the couch.
She will invite you to sit down on the chair beside her."

The President speaks to me about AIDS –
The ungraspable magnitude of the scale of AIDS.
"In the hospital in Lusaka in Zambia
35 per cent of the mothers will die of AIDS."

V

The army officer tells the President that her time is up.
The Bosnia-Herzegovina group is waiting to meet her.
My father picks his own way down the steps,
Alone again in the universe.

He stops the car under a chestnut tree bristling
With growths of conkers – olive sputniks –
Opens up the boot, starts to undress.
I try to stop him but he is without fear or shame.

No rhyme nor reason why he should change his clothes.
Perhaps he is changing his clothes
Because he thinks the President is changing her clothes?
Who knows? It is the way he likes to do things
As, forty years ago, outside the town of Ballina
He used stop at Attymas and change his clothes;
As I myself when I am playing
Like to change my clothes.

Under the chestnut trees in the Phoenix Park
At 11.17 on the last day of August
I look around and stare at my father –
A red deer standing sideways to the car.
I drive out through the Castleknock gate
And stop at Myo's pub in Castleknock village.
I walk in and ask for a cup of coffee.
The barman says without looking up from his business
"And how are the red deer this morning
On the last day of August?"

IV

Women with mops and buckets are washing down the pub.
The barman picks his way across the wet, gleaming floor,
Puts down his tray on my table. He stands over me
Rubbing the back of my neck, stroking my nose,
Feeding my thick, wet, steaming, dribbling lips
With crisps and peanuts.
I click my hooves on the floor.
Through shut lips he mutters, "Not to worry."
Doing my best not to bleat or bellow
I ask him his name.
He takes a deep breath:
"Nijinsky when I am alive," he confides,
Skimming a tabletop with his teatowel
"Nijinsky when I am alive."

VI

"So you met the President!"
Mother roars when I get home.
Why is Mother always roaring?
If only Mother would stop roaring.
If only John, Bill, Gerry, Ian, David would stop roaring.
If only everybody in the world would stop roaring.
What use is a minute's silence? No use.
Let gales peter out into massed snowdrops.
If only the world would be quiet and watch it.

That Douce Woman Who Was Your Neighbour

Because I require this Sunday morning
To be a doing-nothing, prayerful few hours
I switch my red bedside phone to "off".
On second thoughts, switch it back to "on".
Frank is counting down for his last week
Of chemotherapy – he might wish to call.
Straightaway the phone goes off like an alarm.
Lifting the receiver, I fumble the ball –
Frank will kill me, he cannot abide fumbling –
I let it drop, snatch it up.
The cord is snarled up in the sheets.
At the other end – darkness.
I cry out: "Hallo!"
Silence – the silence of parks at night.
All the city parks of Europe howling at night.
The voice is succinct, susurrant:
"This is Jean Smith. Are you free
To join us for a little pasta this evening?
It will be quiet but – not too quiet."

Meeting the Patriarch, Meeting the Ambassador

It was in the Good Old Days in Russia.
September, 1986, Moscow, Patriarch's Ponds.
Three men on a bench guzzling apricot juice.
The chief putting me in the hands of my KGB minder –
Arkadi, a stocky part-Uzbeki part-Russian
With a nasal, oily American accent.
For six weeks in Georgia, Armenia, Uzbekistan, Azerbaijan
Arkadi would guide me on my tour of the Union.

In Tbilisi, Georgia I asked to meet the Patriarch,
His Beatitude and Holiness Ilya II.
Short of turning his Magnum on me, Arkadi
Did everything to prevent such a meeting.
But after three days of silences and threats
A private meeting took place at the Patriarch's villa.
The Patriarch, his secretary, myself and Arkadi.

The Patriarch sitting at the head of the mahogany table
Began the meeting with a formal address.
He asked: What is a poet?
A poet – he said – is an ambassador
Who is the carrier of the significant messages
Across frontiers, checkpoints, walls, controls.

We conversed for an hour and a half
On war and peace, Georgia and Ireland.
Even the gross heart of Arkadi was melted down.
Afterwards he got drunk on Georgian champagne

And praised the Patriarch as an exemplar
Of freedom of religion under Soviet Communism.
But it was to be another eight years
Before I met the Ambassador – before
I deciphered the import of the Patriarch.

In the home of a water-besotted composer in Ranelagh, Dublin,
The composer introduced me to the American Ambassador . . .
Four hours later, down on the docks,
As I walked the deserted banks of the River Liffey,
Along Pigeon House Road up to the East Link Toll Bridge,
Keeping an eye on a stocky man scuttling behind me
In a check bomber jacket and a jockey cap,
A newspaper rolled up in his fist like a policeman's truncheon,
Leaning on the pier rail at the Gut opposite the Point Depot,
My dancing-from-the-cold feet reflected in the lamplit river,
As I watched the night skies over the Phoenix Park,
Terrible black cumuli swirling eastwards across white voids,
I caught glimpses of Ilya II and Jean Kennedy Smith
Huddled together on a streetcorner in Belfast;
In the background Angelo Roncalli and Muhammad Ali –
     ambassadors all.
What is an ambassador?
One who dares wade flooded rivers, carrying a child –
The only child who has the only message.

American Ambassador Going Home

Cut to three thousand feet above the Phoenix Park,
One lemon-yellow light in the blacked-out residence
Of the Ambassador of the United States of America –
Blueprint for a *New Yorker* cover cartoon.

Cut to bedroom interior, the Ambassador abed,
Her eyes closed, her taut pale face tilted,
An open book lying face upwards in her hands,
Angela's Ashes by Frank McCourt:
A Goya *dona* in her veils of sleep.
Energy, exhaustion; pools emptying, filling.
Her birds in their cages; cage-doors left open.

Cut to deserted, walled carpark:
Three of us locking horns in the eyes
Of the video camera on the wall
And of the moon in the Scots pine.
All of us with fanged, discordant versions
Of our native country and of the war in the North.
All of us after four-and-a-half hours
In the company of Jean Kennedy Smith – all of us
Drained of the additives of prejudice;
Protein-injected with information we can trust;
All of us high from having been brushed against
Not only by the black labrador of reality
But by the budgerigars of poetry
Which in a douce woman's stark and sedate chamber
Twit the daylights out of great men in long pants –
Dasvidanyas that swoop behind your ears
Or *spasibas*

That dig their fingernails into your padded shoulders
Or *karashos*
That frisk you up against the walls of time.
What is poetry?
The art of being informal in a formal setting –
Of slipping aboard a Russian yacht without being noticed.
The poet hosts the wild animals of her poem.

Cut to the Butt

Two guys lit up my century.
Mr Michael Carr of Achill Island.
Ms Jean Smith of New York City.
Cut to the butt.

President Robinson Pays Homage to Francis Stuart, 21 October 1996

Let Erin remember the days of old
Ere her faithless sons betray'd her;
When Malachi wore the Collar of Gold,
Which he won from her proud invader.

THOMAS MOORE

This morning at 70 Merrion Square –
The Arts Council of the Republic of Ireland –
President Robinson placed the Collar of Gold
Around the neck of the writer Francis Stuart.
Paying homage to Mr Stuart, the President –
Urgently speaking without a script –
Stated that in the shaping of her own life
Mr Stuart's *Black List, Section H* had played a crucial role;
It had taught her the role of the individual in history:
"His is an awkward, uncomfortable voice."
In response, Mr Stuart, greeting the President,
Stated that as a citizen of Windy Arbour
He felt honoured and proud.
A relaxed President relaxing at Mr Stuart's side
Posed for photographs with the ninety-four-year-old writer.
It was a day when humility scored a gleeful triumph;
Snatched victory from the jaws of spite.

The Functions of the President

There cannot be concord without differences.
NICHOLAS OF CUSA

President Sean T. O'Kelly liked to attend "functions".
That's what he called them – "functions".
His friends called him "Functions O'Kelly".
"I've got a function to go to" he'd inform the wife.
"Functions" were formal occasions
At which formal fellows got formally flutered.

While all around them the emergent
Bourgeoisie of Ballina in the 1950s
Was floundering in Killala Bay
In rowboats of alcohol
Devoid of life jackets,
Missing oars,
Missing rowlocks,
The Bourkes were a functional family.
One of five of a functional family
Mary Bourke married a functional man.
The cartoonist, Mr Nicholas Robinson.

When thirty years later Mrs Robinson was elected
President of the Republic of Ireland
She became head of a dysfunctional family
Numbering between three and four million
Traumatized adolescent parents and children,
Traumatized by alcohol, murder, rhetoric, greed.

Transplanting her own functional background
Into the dysfunctional foreground
Mary Robinson née Bourke injected the blood politic
With serum of justice;
A woman with no fear of hypodermics.
For seven years as Head of State
She teemed the potatoes
Until each potato was hot, gleaming, dry as a floury cake;
Attending to the rights and duties
Of the individual vis-à-vis society.
Between the family and the family members
She induced concord – the undreamed-of concord.
Shaking hands with Gerry Adams
In the Rupert Stanley College in West Belfast.
Shaking hands with David Ervine
In the Irish consulate in New York.
Shaking hands with Anthony McDonnell in his pinstripe
    pyjamas
Sitting up in bed in the new AIDS unit in St James's Hospital.
No, not *shaking* hands with Anthony –
Clasping hands with Anthony, hand over hand.
"All the children of the nation will be cherished equally."

And but then! – and but how! – we repaid her!
In '97 we staged a presidential election
In which we defiled the status of women.
In her stead we elected the Celtic Elk
Whose hooves are the hooves of a hairy economy;
The superfluous span of whose antlers cannot penetrate
The Scots pines of our ancient songlines;
Under the shredded umbrella spokes of whose fossil tines
The children of the nation are no longer children
But Barbie dinosaurs in chains dragging aborted dreams.
From the functional years of the 1990s
We are crashing into the twenty-first century,

The digitally manipulated, pixelated panorama of 2001:
Into the virtual instead of the actual
Shells on Rosses' level shore.
At heel, at heel; conform, conform.
The formality of spontaneity is dead;
The chaos of cliché has succeeded.

Mary Robinson née Bourke, stay where you are
In Africa or South America or Southeast Asia.
Dream, we dream – we've got you in our bloodstream –
Of unique spirals, abstract, functional;
As Ireland was in 3500 BC
And became again AD 1990.
O functional woman whom no gods destroy!

The Mary Robinson Years

The just shall flourish like the palm tree
Psalm 91:13

I

In November 1990 Mary Robinson lit a candle in her window
For all the exiles of the Irish diaspora.
Seven years later Mary threw her farewell party
In the Copacabana Palace Hotel
On the seafront in Rio – a gem of art deco;
Her husband Nick being an architectural historian
Has a professional interest in art deco
And in any case that's where Mary happened to be
And she thought it would be an agreeable idea
If we all flew out to Rio to join her –
Bride and Luke and Barbara and Enda and Ann and all the gang.

It was a fireworks night in Rio.
All the men as well all the ladies
Came in smart, casual attire.
The best of champagne, wine, rum.
Motivated conversation
Bejewelled with serious
Humour of the right kind.
Fernando Henrique
Attended with Ruthie.

That the party had helicoptered
Over Corcovado –
The Statue of Christ the King

254

Far below us on its hill top
Overseeing Rio and the sea –
Ignited theological controversy
A propos liberation theology;
The nexus, if any,
Between inequality
And the Ascension into Heaven;
What Leonardo Boff called
"The aerodynamics of injustice".
Amidst the rocks of his own laughter
The curly, grey, apostle-like Boff cried out:
"Bearded in my own den –
Danton amongst the Robespierres!"

The only other jarring note
Was that although
I was seated opposite Mary
I could not get a word in.
In fact, I could not
Make eye contact with Mary.
If I didn't know Mary
I might have thought
She was snubbing me.
But then suddenly at the end
She caught my eye:
"Black eye, Paul?"
I blushed puce.
"No, no, no, no – "
I cried, rubbing the red
Bruise under my right eye –
"That's my birthmark.
Keeps getting me into deep water!"

It was a palmy night
Outside the Copacabana Palace Hotel.
The most stunning woman I have ever set eyes on in my life —
Six foot tall, mulatto, red hair down to her hips —
Stepped right up to me,
Whipped up her T-shirt
To show me her incredible breasts,
 Whipped it down again.

She said: "Don't faint, darling.
I'm a transvestite and
You won't believe this but
I'm from Tipperary."
I said: "Oh!
Whereabouts in Tipperary
Are you from?"
"Killenaule" — she smiled — "Killenaule."
I said: "What are you doing in Copacabana?"
"My night off" — she smiled — "my night off!
I'm an NGO relief aid worker.
Faith and good works and all that.
The Gospel according to Saint Matthew."
She added: "What are you doing here?"
I said: "I'm a friend of Mary Robinson's."
She said: "Oh you're not!
Only a friend?"

She turned her smouldering spine on me
And strode off into the night of Rio,
The gigantic, ocean waves of the South Atlantic
Breaking in rainbows of fireworks behind her.
It was midnight, September 1, 1997 —

High time to get down on my knees
And to light a candle in the sand,
Cupping a flame in my hand.

Only a friend
Cupping a flame in my hand.